The
Garland Library
of
War and Peace

The
Garland Library
of
War and Peace

Under the General Editorship of

Blanche Wiesen Cook, *John Jay College, C.U.N.Y.*

Sandi E. Cooper, *Richmond College, C.U.N.Y.*

Charles Chatfield, *Wittenberg University*

War Dance
A Study of the Psychology of War

by
Eric Graham Howe

with a new introduction
for the Garland Edition by
Elise Boulding

Garland Publishing, Inc., New York & London
1972

Library of Congress Cataloging in Publication Data

Howe, Eric Graham, 1897-
  War dance.

  (Garland library of war and peace)
  Reprint of the 1937 ed.
  1. War--Psychological aspects. I. Title.
II. Series.
U22.3.H68 1972   155.9'35   74-147471
ISBN 0-8240-0263-6

Printed in the United States of America

Introduction

"There are only two possible gestures about life,"
wrote Graham Howe in 1937, "the closed fist and the
open palm. . . . Between these two, history repeats
itself." This two-dimensional dialectic is achingly
familiar to both peace scholars and peace activists in
the 1970s, as closed fists and open palms continually
move past each other in the melee of liberation
struggles that hopelessly scramble these concepts of
peace, freedom, and social justice that were so tidily
organized in the previous century's rhetoric about the
unity of humankind.

As we struggle to free ourselves from the trap of
that two-dimensional dialectic, it is particularly
timely to rediscover the writings of a British
psychologist who understood the nature of the trap
well before the current social movements began.
"Life is conflict" is the basic premise of Howe's
book. Using that as a springboard, he plunges into
waters only somewhat less uncharted now than when
he first wrote, bypassing all familiar channels and
landmarks for the sake of an unprogrammed view of
the ocean of life. Determined to free the mind from
conventional dialectical thinking, he actually comes
up with an "operationalized" four-dimensional
metaphysic, thus out-McCluhaning McCluhan and

5

out-Aquarianing the Aquarians. The third dimension he adds with his charmingly outrageous diagrams that range in style from the flower-like mandala to Indian picture-writing with stick figures. The fourth dimension comes through the rendition of dreams that remain stubbornly untranslated, yet stubbornly relevant, to the concepts he is communicating. Howe wants the book to stick in our throats. He says so (p. 21). And it does. The mood in which to read it is the mood of the disciple of a Zen master who has been given a particularly difficult koan on which to meditate.

"What is war?" asks Howe. A noxious weed in humanity's garden. Who are the sowers of the noxious weed? We, the gardeners. We plant the first seeds of disaster in the nursery, when we treat the new-born infant as a bundle of potentially undesirable behavior. From there on we continue sowing everywhere in the family, the school room, the church, the law court, bank, place of work — wondering all the time where the weeds come from. The irony is that all these seeds are sown with good intentions. This is because the problem of war is the problem of life itself. As we deal with the conflicts within ourselves and the conflicts outside ourselves, in the ordinary course of daily life, we continuously trigger sequences that lead to fatal oppositions instead of fruitful combinations, in the society around us. This is not a necessary feature of the human condition, however, says Howe. The purpose

INTRODUCTION

of his book is to help us distinguish between the war of life, which is the very stuff of our existence, and man's war, which is a consequence of our failure to deal with the dialectical nature of reality in its entirety.

The dualities of light and shade, up and down, give and take, continually defeat our straight-arrow approach to life tasks. The laws of four-dimensional logic contradict the evidence of our senses, so that life moves, not in a straight line, but round and round. Howe anticipates the counter-culture's rediscovery of yin and yang by thirty years, pointing out that the East has known what Christianity has ignored for 2,000 years, that one does not obtain "good" fruit by eliminating "evil" roots. The book is essentially devoted to enabling the Western-trained mind to hold polarities in a fluid state within the consciousness, without structuring them according to previously acquired mental habits. At the strictly cognitive level we could say he is aiming at what Else Frenkel-Brunswick called "ambiguity tolerance," in an area well explored by Festinger in his Theory of Cognitive Dissonance.[1] *But he is at the same time dealing with a transcendence of the contradictions in the self; the concept of self-actualization developed by A. H. Maslow* [2] *perhaps comes closest to what Howe is driving at. But he draws on more than psychology. In his concern to liberate the disciplined mind from the disaster-potentiating patterns it habitually follows, the author is continually bringing in the psycho-social situation in which the individual acts, sociology continually creeps in, though not in easily recognizable language.*

Howe's unique brand of social psychology will best be understood by taking time to ponder the 28 diagrams that illuminate the psycho-social dilemmas generated by the internal and external polarities and flows that humans must deal with. The message the diagrams convey is that "choosing, we must choose wrongly" (p. 300). In a succession of representations of root versus flower, immobility versus flight, containment versus expansion, inner versus outer, always the little stick figures are shown either as pushed/pulled by the dualities, or anchored in a secure nth dimension at the core of the dualities.

I feel I ought to say something about the role of the dream narrations in the complex non-structure of the book. This is hard to do. The best I can come up with is that they seem to be intended to unsettle the mind in case the reader has been arriving at some premature and simplistic conclusions about what the author is trying to say.

The pithy text, often aphoristic, the diagrams and the dreams, all point to an image of a new human who has fearlessly submitted himself to pain as a teacher in the exploration of the love-hate relationship man has with himself and the cosmos. The new human emerges from that experience able to act in society with a new grace. Like Karen Horney,[3] Lawrence Frank,[4] and Abram Kardiner,[5] who were

INTRODUCTION

all writing at about that time, Howe sees society itself as essentially neurosis-producing, and he looks to a new type of person whose perceptions and behaviors will not be subject to distortion by cultural pressures. Even more than that, he sees the new person as able to redeem neurosis-inducing social structures and role expectations, secure in the knowledge of a transcendent wholeness that encompasses fragmented human experience. This liberated man, freed from excessive dependence on property and status, inoculated against the passions of consumerism that poison the body social, will look neither to systems nor messiahs to save his planet, but to his own capacity for relationship with his fellow humans. The frenetic rituals of the war dance will be replaced by the free-swinging grace of a peace dance. Today's student generation will say, "Right on!"

The people to whom this book was addressed in the thirties were the intent and upwardly mobile working men and women and housewives who have filled the classrooms of the adult education movement for a good part of this century. The chapters were prepared as lectures in a series on war and peace under the auspices of the Home and School Council in London in 1936 and 1937, as the war clouds were gathering in Europe. This fact gives added poignancy to his efforts to show men and women how to draw on their humanness to create a dance of peace. One wonders how they heard what he said! Perhaps because of the nature of the audience, there are no references to the works of other psychologists, or to scientists of any kind. The lectures however, draw widely on psychological concepts current at the time. With the added spice of his own creative mind Howe managed to anticipate many of the developments of the sixties and now the seventies. Perhaps the nearest equivalent to Howe's book today, in terms of dealing with the creation of the new human using the ingredients of the old, is Charles Hampden-Turner's Radical Man.[6] *The latter is much more scholarly and makes more explicit the sociological dimension implicit in Howe. Also, it is thoroughly documented where Howe is free of footnotes. The imaginative use of concepts and diagrams, the treatment of polarities and conflicts as a purging fire from which the new man arises, Phoenix-like, are however, common to both. Each book illuminates the other, and reassures us that knowledge may after all be cumulative. T. S. Eliot speaks for both:*

> The dove descending breaks the air
> With flame of incandescent terror
> Of which the tongues declare
> The one discharge from sin and error
> The only hope, or else despair,
> Lies in the choice of pyre or pyre
> To be redeemed from fire by fire.[7]

Elise Boulding
University of Colorado

INTRODUCTION

NOTES

[1] *L. Festinger*, Theory of Cognitive Dissonance *(Evanston, Ill.: Row Petersen, 1957).*

[2] *A. H. Maslow*, Toward a Psychology of Being *(Princeton, New Jersey: D. Van Nostrand and Company, 1962).*

[3] *Karen Horney*, Neurotic Personality of Our Time *(New York: W. W. Norton, 1937).*

[4] *Lawrence Frank*, Society As the Patient *(Port Washington, N.Y.: Kennikat Press, Inc., 1969).*

[5] *Abram Kardiner, et. al.*, Psychological Frontiers of Society *(New York: Columbia University Press, 1945).*

[6] *Charles Hampden-Turner*, Radical Man *(New York: Schenkman Publishing Company, 1970).*

[7] *T. S. Eliot*, Four Quartets *(New York: Harcourt, Brace and World, 1943), p. 37.*

11

WAR DANCE

WAR DANCE

A Study of
The Psychology of War

by

E. GRAHAM HOWE
M.B., B.S. (Lond.), D.P.M.

FABER & FABER LIMITED
24 Russell Square
London

First Published in April Mcmxxxvii
by Faber and Faber Limited
24 Russell Square London W.C.1
Printed in Great Britain by
Latimer Trend & Co Ltd Plymouth

To

NORA

'Among the first habits that a young architect should learn, is that of thinking in shadow.'
—RUSKIN: *The Stones of Venice*

'The mystery of life is not a problem to be solved, it is a reality to be experienced.'
—J. J. VAN DE LEEUW: *The Conquest of Illusion*

'Religion is the transition from God the void to God the enemy and from God the enemy to God the companion.'
—A. N. WHITEHEAD: *Religion in the Making*

'The world order is a harmony of opposing tensions—as in the Lyre and the Bow.'
—HERACLITUS

CONTENTS

DIAGRAMS

DIAGRAMS

DREAMS

DIAGRAM 1

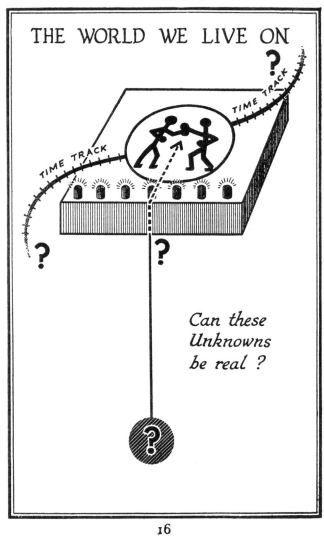

THE WORLD WE LIVE ON

TIME TRACK

TIME TRACK

Can these
Unknowns
be real ?

Introduction

In the autumn of 1936 I was asked by the Home &
School Council to give an introductory course of six
lectures on Peace and War. I was all the more glad to
do so because of the enforced clearing of my mind on
the matter. I became increasingly aware, however, of
multiplied evidences of impending disaster. I wondered whether so much should be said, or how it could
be said without being unduly rude about the organization of society. It does no one any good to hit a man
when he is down; yet can he be stood upon his feet
again? The answer to that question was: let's see. The
lectures were duly given, with the aid of Study Groups,
and the subject matter was subsequently translated
into book form. But although I always enjoy the task
of writing, I cannot help envying a real author his
liberty of time, for none of this has been either planned
or written during lawful working hours.[1]

. . . . .

How old, we may wonder, is this human race to
which we belong? Is it still pre-adolescent on the scale

[1] The lectures were repeated (four instead of six) at the
Conway Hall, London, in February and March 1937.

of History, and shall we in some thousands of years grow out of this rough habit of rudeness and fisticuffs? Or are we so old as to be drivelling into senile decay, digging our graves as we topple unsteadily into the unseen? We have lived a long time: long enough to learn much, perhaps too much. But we have not yet learnt how to live. It must be difficult, then, this task of living. The problem of aggressiveness, of peace or war, is the problem of all time. How is it to be solved? We feel we must have an answer now, or perish.

But why are we so aggressively insistent upon an answer? Why this blackmail upon reason, that we must be told at once, or the consequences will be most threatening? It is a little childish to insist upon one more answer, seeing that we already suffer from an inconsistent plethora of pious and hopeful inaccuracies. There are far too many answers already; that is at least part of the trouble.

Whatever errors there may be in the following pages, this book does not profess to answer questions. The most it claims to do is to throw a little light upon the questioner, that he may stop to look, wondering a little, forgetting his vicious habit of forcing answers into all the silent spaces of the unseen. There is no answer to the question that is Life; but that answer will not yet settle his false hopes.

The rhythm of life has become a broken melody, because, given the freedom and the right to choose, we have picked out only the white notes upon the scale, seeing so sensibly that they must be best. Thus, according to our egotistic anthem, lines must be straight. The best ones go forever upwards, up and up and up, in one ecstatic note transcendent, overwhelming all differences in vainglorious victory. Thus would we beat the rhythmic time of more courageous life, which swings upon a curve, generously including both the black notes and the white, the silence and the sound.

In first and last analysis, there are only two possible gestures about life. These are the closed fist and the open palm, meaning tension and relaxation. Between these two, history repeats itself. Amidst infinite variety, this is the simplest analysis of bilateral division, which may be symbolized mathematically as plus and minus. This is the basis of the mystic law 'As for one, so for all; as above, so below'. This is the root of all analysis, and is expressed in the diagram of relationship, one circle within another, for nucleus and protoplasm, self and circumstance, or nation and neighbours. This much of relativity remains the same for all: that they can each behave by 'Yes' or 'No'. Rooted so deep, here is the universal law in stark simplicity.

Unfortunately it is most complicated, because all the worst errors of mankind in judgment arise precisely out of such a bilateral classification into This and That. Seeing that 'This is better than That', it is so plain to see that 'That' ought to become 'This', or go. Mankind readily adopts this attitude of martial negative and buccaneering morality; but there is also the opposite attitude of more positive and peaceful acceptance of this basic duality of life. Not ought, but is; not negative, but positive; not morality, but reality; indeed, why not let be?

So this is the point: the metaphysic of so simple a

duality is a hopeless fallacy, devastatingly dangerous, for it is not complete. To express the whole truth, we require not measures thus upon only two dimensions, but at least upon four. The mere alternative to error is not enough to make error into truth, e.g. if action itself is wrong, it is also wrong to assume that inaction is any better. We must discover another opposing couple to that of action-inaction, which will be more true to life. The metaphysic which is true to life without a fault, indeed the only one, is that of the double duality, or cruciform pattern, if we can but make it move. In this case the four is very different from the double of the two.

It is this metaphysic which provides the logic of the following pages. Simplicity may at times be deceptive. Similarity may omit to notice difference. Complexity may suggest confusion ('how he does run on'). Mixed metaphors may imply a muddled mind. Diagrams may just mean laziness. But let us not forget that there is this subtle difference between the three-dimensional and the four-dimensional metaphysic, that in spite of apparent similarity they are also related to one another as foreign languages. Being so different, it is a pity that they should look so much the same, because it is inevitable that the one will be blamed by some for not being the other. Yet, since we are the kind of people that we are, that cannot be helped.

The different angle of another vision finds a useful medium in diagrams and dreams. It is the habit of consciousness to produce a convenient fiction of drama drawn out into a straight line, according to the pattern which begins at the beginning 'Once upon a time . . .'

and ends at the end 'so they lived (un)happily ever after'. This pattern is shared both by History and Fairy Tales. Even dreams appear thus spun into a single thread, when pulled out straight by consciousness; but where they belong, in sleep, they weave a more complex web. They live like diagrams across a space, related parts moving in breadth, height and depth, without that fallacy of the first word and the last, until consciousness proves they ought to have a beginning, an end, a middle, and (of course!) a purpose. Before each chapter a dream thus stands to speak its part, as oracle, in puzzle pictures; with, at the end, an appendix offering some comment, with apology for allowing so much deference to querulous curiosity.

Yet it is with consciousness that you will read this book, according to its way, which is not in accordance with the other laws of sleep. A word of warning, then: don't force the frame of thought to fit over and include something which may not be the same. Allow for difference, and do not force understanding defensively to consume a certain waywardness, provocative, disturbing, from a source unseen.

There are some puzzles here, to be left as open questions, ever. The value of diagrams is that they transcend the limits of the written word. They may not be so accurate, yet for that reason they are the more provoking. The reader feels annoyed, irritated that here is something which withstands his swift assault. We read so greedily that it is good thus to have something that sticks in our mental throats a while, doing something to us perhaps, instead of only being done to death.

INTRODUCTION

Need there be apologies for dreams, which are so true to life, yet so untrue to the lesser principle of consciousness? How can we be sure of dreams, what do they mean? We may ask the same question of Life itself, and hesitate long before we answer.

Why must we be so sure? It does seem difficult to let things be. Yet dreams are products of a growth, like flowers. A creative act of some divine unseen, they are often ridiculed, as are many other priceless gifts, and laughed at by rude boys whose self-assurance is the best proof that their ignorance has been both fixed and satisfied. They are so sure of their superiority; but

> *Dreamer of dreams! We take the taunt with gladness,*
> *Knowing that time, beyond the years you see,*
> *Hath wrought the dreams which count with you for*
> *madness*
> *Into the substance of the life to be.*

E. G. H.

146 Harley Street, W.1.
March 1937

CHAPTER I: VICIOUS CIRCLE

SUMMARY

Dreams.

Terms. Words are weapons; essential and inessential difference; pegs for fixing; intolerable suspense.

Curved or Straight Lines. The meaning of metaphysics; X 3 and X 4; dimensional differences; life needs X 4.

Two Modes of Thinking. Cognitive and conative, moving and fixed. Anxiety and action; humour and perspective.

Seeds of War. Where is the cause? The error of good intentions; we are the gardeners who grow the weed of war.

Inward Conflict. We are two selves; how can we be made one?

The Self-Important Self. Perspective and proportion; what is mine is best, or ought to be.

Genesis. A tale of separation; the umbilical cord; weaning; the 'ought' of unity.

Yang and Yin. 5000 years ago; the X 4 metaphysic of accepted duality; Christianity and false teaching; the eradicated root.

Metaphysics, Science and Medicine. The effect of a wrong

23

metaphysic; the error of isolation; ignorance of the unseen.

The Privilege of Choice. St. George and the Dragon; attitude to evil; East and West.

Diagrams. Poles apart; The River; The All-round Man.

DREAMS[1]

I. '*The Learned Knife*'

I was given a most delicious looking pear, which was so juicy it made my mouth water. I cut it open with a knife and was very disappointed to find that one half of it was black, and I thought it must be bad. I cut it open and was horrified to find a worm inside, so that I threw it away.

I was relieved to think that I had at least the other half, but when I cut that in two, I found another little worm. I then cut it all into small pieces, but at the centre of each I found there was a worm.

II. '*Contrast*'

I was walking along with someone vague in the open country with the sea in the distance. It was a gloriously warm and sunny day. I must have been indoors before, because I said: 'I don't think there is anything worse than having to be indoors on a day like this.' I felt it was such a pity that so many people did not seem to care.

Then I was in an underground, a sort of hall place, full of smoke, darkness and gloom, and I felt the contrast very keenly. There was a girl there whom I knew,

[1] For comment, see Appendix (page 305).

very white and unhealthy looking, but really she is a very healthy, active and outdoor sort of person. Although I felt that it was a great mistake for her to be there, I felt that I could never make her see the difference. I seemed to be patting myself on the back for knowing so much better than she did.

Chapter I

VICIOUS CIRCLE

Different Terms

Words are the tools of argument and may lead to war. Although useful to define accurate meaning, they may become aggressive and mischievous weapons, saying what we do not mean, and causing unnecessary misunderstanding. In fact, most misunderstandings are due to words; therefore since we speak our feelings, we must learn to read between these lines of words, interpreting them to see what they may mean. So many people use the same words with quite different meanings; or indeed, without much idea as to the meanings that they do intend, especially if the word is a short one of common speech, such as 'love' or 'peace'.

Much of our difference is only about inessential matters, such as the words themselves in which the difference and similarity are veiled. This kind of difference, which is the more superficial, can usually be overcome when we meet together in the lecture-room, or round the dinner or conference table.

There are differences, however, which are not of this inessential kind. They are fundamental, differences of type and character which, if justice is to be done, must thus be left. This is not that; woman is not man; I am not you; France is not Germany; Buddhism is not Christianity. For the sake of justice it must be understood that that word 'not' is a protective barrier which prevents the one from overrunning the proper limits of the other, thereby frustrating its liberties, interfering with its rights and eventually obliterating it for the sake of a supremacy of one half of the argument. It is a guarantor of peace, to be respected.

Differences there must be between writer and reader, in which the reader, wisely enough, will hesitate, seeking to qualify and sometimes to contradict. In all the pages that follow a policy will be maintained, worked out from different points of view, repeated possibly somewhat repetitively. It is hoped, however, that differences between writer and reader will be maintained as such and not hastily abandoned, for there is much virtue in this agreement upon difference. Although there are some who when they read must agree or disagree with every word that any author writes, these are not those for whom this book is written. Let there be difference. Across that friendly gulf let us define ourselves and move, making friendly contact in the study of these beloved enemies.

There may be many points of difference, varying from a criticism of the argument as unnecessarily complicated, to another that the illustrations are ridiculously simple. In regard to these diagrams, there may be much disagreement, for there are many people who are not sympathetic with the method of diagrammatic presentation. This is used again, however, because it seems to have a particularly fruitful contribution to make to the whole subject of the four-dimensional metaphysic, which requires some method of thus portraying symbolically the whole relatedness of space and time. It is easy to fix words, not realizing that we are deceiving ourselves by doing so. It is comparatively difficult to fix these diagrams without feeling foolish, because when they are fixed they mean nothing, which annoys some readers who are inclined too hastily to grasp and understand, and may be why they so dislike them. If our attitude is 'I must know at once', then a diagram is of no use, because it can only act to delay the process of a false assumption. It is a seed to be planted in the mind, to grow or not in time according to the soil.

These diagrams are not recommended for their æsthetic advantages, but only for this uncertain fruitful simplicity with which they may be possessed, for those who approach them with a seeing eye. The reader should be warned against trying to do anything with them. He should wait and see what they do to him. The diagram belongs to a method of life and movement that occasionally amplifies the halting and anxious flow of the written word.

There are many differences in life, which makes for interest as well as argument. But there are those who for the sake of peace would try to argue them away, overcoming the resistance which that word 'not' indicates, rolling two different meanings into one in an aggressive effort to make effective compromise. In doing so, they say that this is for the sake of peace, and feel pleased that all are now agreed. Having found a 'formula', they try to bind this peace with promissory notes and peace treaties. Thus, by confining a just difference, they tell us that at least for a period we are assured of peace.

But are we in fact any better off for having used living words as pegs, to fix that which must move if it is to be real and live? Surely we might as well try to confine water within the confines of a leaky sieve, as thus to change the laws of difference by wordy arguments and scraps of paper. Peace that depends on scraps of paper can be torn up at any moment. It will be consumed (without surprise to those who are wise to the facts of life) by the first friction which occurs, stricken into flame by the living tinder of emotional relationships. There are things we can and things we cannot do with words, and we must learn to recognize and respect our occasional impotence.

Now here is the rub; there seems to be some inherent unwillingness in human nature to face the anxiety and tension of an unresolved state of difference. We do not like suspense, it seems intolerable. 'I am NOT you', but I do not like that 'not' between us, for it means that you are unknown to me. I would like you to be known and fixed, but you are moving; and much of you, at least one half, is unseen, however carefully I keep my eye on you. Our experience of life in reality is thus limited, relative. This situation of relationship is one of movement and uncertainty. Our habit then, as we swiftly seek to resolve this problem and escape suspense, is to eliminate the movement and to obtain some firm fixation if we can. We feel sure that this situation of unrest, this strain and unbearable uncertainty should not be; we ought to be one, at rest. Evidently we are divided, but it seems to us self-evident that we ought not to be. And so we try to fix aggressively, for our security, what life would move with unseen hand.

The better to ease anxiety and escape from fear of the unknown, with words or phrases, forms or formulæ, we try to fix this moving spirit of our lives and say: 'Let there be peace.' But alas! it cannot be done so easily, and we are soon all at sea again, pitched from the platform of our hopes into that stirring scene of conflict which is life. The waters rise and fall, the storm threatens us with drowning and it seems so reasonable that we should attempt to save the frail barque of self with this appeal for peace. Of course, we must have peace! But is peace thus to be bought at the price of life itself—at the price of fixation, where life is movement? Perhaps even death is movement also, and we may be right to feel that peace, which is bought at the price of this fixation out of fear, may be something worse than death.

Tired of our conflict, urgently desiring peace, we long for the safety of some system, although we know quite well how systems have failed in the past, whether in our own hands or in those of others. We long for knowledge, because we are afraid of ignorance, fearing that in this unseen there may be some hidden threat to deprive us of our much desired security. We feel afraid and run away from life. We cannot agree to differ, but must decide by argument—this or that—and heads or tails, who wins? Surely there must be something, somewhere, which is *all* right—so why should that not be our egotistic selves?

Therefore some of us back horses and some back systems; but no one wins for long. It seems as if Life has always something up its sleeve, unseen, to take us by surprise. It seems as if it is possessed of something which we, from our limited standpoint, cannot contend with or control. There is always something beyond us, something more that seems to make all the difference, defeating all our plans. Life seems to be moving on a curve, although we always try to fix it straight, because it seems to us it would be better so. This can but lead to endless argument and hopeless conflict, for in the end life must win and our straight lines must go.

Curved or Straight Lines

But can we come to terms with these same curves, thinking in them and with them, instead of against them? It is the contention of this book that consciousness and reason can be so developed as to cope more effectively with life, if we can but learn a better method, a truer metaphysic, and more living language. We need not feel that it is necessary to give up hope, whilst fighting blindly against unseen forces which must defeat us in the end. Our blindness has been due to faulty method which, if we improve it, can again put us in a position of power to manifest that essential life force, drawing from it our inspiration and our very selves. Life cannot really be our enemy; but if we are to be as friends, we must learn to respect and obey its laws and our limitations.

What is this one thing more which, if it escapes us, leaves us so hopelessly disappointed; yet, if we had it in our minds and in our methods, would enable us to keep control over those difficult circumstances in which we have to live? During the course of the following chapters, the same theme will be developed in systematic fashion, for here is a system; yet not that system which would fix, but one which moves. When analysed, each to their respective poles and separated by a friendly negative, we can define two different systems, two possible metaphysical approaches or conceptual languages, which also correspond to two widely separated attitudes towards life. This difference may be stated from the start. Namely, one system of thought aims at eliminating movement and is thus the system which is responsible for all aggressiveness and war; whereas the other recognizes the primacy of movement, and is the mode of thought which must be acquired as habit, before peace can be developed and maintained amongst mankind. For purposes of labels, these two systems are called on the one hand the 'three-dimensional metaphysic' and on the other the 'four-dimensional metaphysic'. (The word 'metaphysic' is not used in any sense to imply an approach to the supernatural, but simply as the word which indicates the first principles of our approach to thought and logical method.)

The claim is made that life, which moves and grows, therefore requires the four-dimensional metaphysic, in spite of the fact that the function of consciousness attempts to pin it within a fixation scheme of three-dimensional limits. Psychology, philosophy, theology, to be adequate to life, all require the four-dimensional metaphysic. Yet it will be seen how meanings change according to these two modes of thought, and the same word will be found to have two different meanings if it is approached as fixed, or as moving. For instance, the word 'peace' according to the four-dimensional metaphysic is possessed of a quality of movement, which is inherent within the situation in which it exists and grows. The same word, however, by the three-dimensional metaphysic is something which has been fixed, made static and therefore dead, and thus inadaptable to the lives of those whom it would so feebly attempt to bind by promises and treaties, boundaries or protective tariffs. The question is, therefore, whether our understanding can be within the laws and limits of a living process; or whether it must be confined in the limits of a fallacious system, which is called either 'politics' or 'economics', 'psychology', 'philosophy' or 'religion'.

Two Modes of Thinking

Here then is the first discipline imposed by the NOT of an analysis. The alternatives for our first contrast are established in this accepted difference, which recognizes that there are these two modes of thought in regard to which we can thus say: This is not That. The first is the mode of 'thought without movement' (Fixation Thinking), in which the force of fear and flight has led to our assumption of some fixed goal, which we must-have now. We must-have peace, because we cannot bear this movement; we must-have security, possessions and knowledge, because we cannot bear the uncertainty of the unknown. We must be sure we understand, for only then can we be sure that all is fixed, that it is good, and that it means peace. Unfortunately, however, that cannot be true, and this way of thinking is the beginning of all conflict, because it is the adoption of an aggressive attitude towards reality.

TWO MODES OF THINKING

Let us contrast this with that other mode of thought, which we may call 'Observation Thinking'. (For those who are interested in orthodox terminology, this may be called 'cognitive thinking' in contrast to the previous mode of thought, the purpose of which was alteration, change, interference, which was 'conative thinking'.) If our process of thought is to be that of observing without trying to alter (i.e. illumination), then our observation is of a moving quality, in regard to which we are limited so that we can only say 'I see', hoping that we may in time see further into the unseen, and yet meanwhile content that so much must still remain unseen. 'Observation Thinking' is a quality of vision that is allied to foresight, but both are usually lacking in the habits of 'fixation thinking' of our political guardians.

The new method is not to go and do, in urgent action in order to alleviate anxiety, but to watch and—if we know the meaning of the word—to watch and pray. Not that we may be safe, but that we may be true to life within ourselves and beyond, amongst those other different selves which form our contacts and relationships. So let us see; which involves the virtue of humility and wonder, facing even fear, and knowing that with all our ignorance we may be wrong. Thus we may agree to differ, feeling content even with our discontent.

Our trouble is neither knowledge nor lack of it, for we have more than enough. In every situation upon which we embark, we are so overloaded with knowledge that this great advantage is in danger of defeating itself. Knowledge has become so much a possession, so much

35

a guardian of security, that we have become fat with it, and the baggage train with which we travel upon life's journey is so heavy that it will hardly move at all. Whatever may be our professional approach to the task of earning a living, as the years go by the amount of knowledge which we must acquire becomes more and more. Those who realize that there is in fact no end to it, must also see that there will come a time when this hunger for the acquisition of more knowledge must cease, having defeated its own end, dying from a surfeit of itself. Our minds nowadays are stored with much knowledge, and our nation is burdened with much wealth and a great empire. But there is much to be said in favour of the mind which is stripped and empty, and for the nation which is still in the infancy of its growth, rather than in the position of established wealth and apparent security. These highly organized imperious structures are a grave responsibility, because there comes a time when growth must fail.

The larger the tree, the larger must be its roots. Yet we behave as if there is some blessed Providence upon whom we can so far rely as to urge the tree to greater and greater harvest, with no more than an occasional flogging of the roots with artificial stimulants. Our three-dimensional metaphysicians, with their urgent anxiety to please themselves, have failed miserably to deal with this vital problem of supply and demand, because they have failed to see the balance, and to obey the law which life itself so clearly manifests. Of knowledge we have more than plenty, but of balance not enough. We must not cheat nor must we live upon false hope, unless we are to prejudice the chances of the next generation, who for our folly must be made to pay.

It is not enough to hope for peace; it is not enough to work for it, if our working amounts only to unwise interference with the laws of nature and experience. We must be prepared to learn unwelcome lessons, to stand on one side and watch without impatience the fall of the castle of our hope, obedient to facts instead of merely anxious to coerce them to suit our own convenience. If there are occasions on which we are faced with difficulties which do not suit our wishes, then by this method of the observant eye our action is limited to a deepening vision, because we must not interfere.

At this point as we watch ourselves, we notice that there is something in our minds which at once starts the question: 'Yes, but if we do not do anything, what is going to happen?' It looks as if we cannot believe that anything will happen unless we are its conscious cause. We have so little faith in Life as the prime mover, cause and law of our being, that we feel it must fail if denied the benefit of our direction. But indeed there is no need to worry about action, for that can always be left to take care of itself; unfortunately, all too soon, for action is cheap enough. It is always so precipitous and hasty. We need not worry about a condition of inertia overcoming us, because there is so much of this intensive urgency to move, even when movement is neither wise nor kind. 'What shall we do about it?' is a question no sooner asked than answered by some urgent action, for anxiety cannot stop long considering. Our politicians and missionaries are easily prompted to a

37

policy of benevolent interference, in order to force change upon those unfortunate enough to differ.

There is so much unctuous moralizing required to support this policy of interference, however, that it seems to indicate that a sense of humour is not to be found within the limits of the three-dimensional metaphysic. It must be supplied ready-made from outside, as jokes to laugh at. This lack is unfortunately true, because humour depends upon balance and movement, and the only thing which the three-dimensional metaphysic is anxious to avoid is change, other than that which is to somebody's personal advantage.

Although there may always be laughter at the heart of things, it is not easy to retain a sense of humour. It is comparatively easy to laugh at other people's jokes, especially if they are well-worn samples of an ancient pattern. We can all laugh when we are happy and when things go well with us, especially with the aid of good company, good food, good alcohol and good cigars. The after-dinner speaker, however, who makes us laugh so heartily may suffer from an intermittent myopia, which makes it quite impossible for him to see beyond the end of his egotistical nose. His speech, although an example of excellent oratory, well filled with the plums of good humour, may be sadly lacking in perspective, as much of his humour is drawn at the expense of making fun of someone else beyond his intellectual horizon. We can all laugh at some things, but there are very few of us who can laugh at everything; and yet the real test of humour would be, not that we can laugh at what is funny, but that we can still laugh when there is nothing funny to laugh at.

THE SEED OF WAR

Anybody can stand up straight when he is not being pushed, but the proof of stability is how to stand a storm. Our good humour is excellent as long as our likes and preferences, our sense of security and self-importance, are not being questioned. But if there is the suggestion of potential difference, in which our cherished prejudices may suffer—whether moral or in more material things—then our good humour and our sense of it is tested. There are not many of us who can laugh when we are being laughed at. Laughter, like charity, begins at home: escaping outwardly in aggressive guffaws, its inward light is often lost.

The Seed of War

If there are 'Mad Dogs' at large in Europe at the present time (but how dangerous are these snappy labels!) it is not enough to ask for guns or chains. Who bit the dog, and why is he so mad? War is an effect, a symptom of disease, a madness grown from many causal roots. There is so much anxiety at the present time to eliminate this awful threat of War, that it is surely wise to consider what has led up to this end result which is now so threatening to our peace of mind, our stability and security. There must be some 'cause' to have produced this situation which is so very far removed from anything which anyone could consciously desire. It is as if we all want peace with most benevolent sincerity, and yet there is this urgent impulse towards War, which nobody wants and nobody can control. Asking for bread we have been given a stone, and we naturally want to know who has betrayed us. Swiftly and externally as is our way, seeking

39

for a 'cause', we point angrily to some 'rascal' whose peaceful intentions, however, have not been so different from our own.

Compelled by the instability of circumstance, and alive at last to danger, we feel that civilization itself is threatened and that all the fruit of our culture may be doomed by this foul weed which threatens to overwhelm all the other plants in our garden. Seeing the situation as we are faced with it now, it looks as if a certain pessimistic school of thought is right, and that peace is not strong enough to stand against the ravages of war. Yet who planted this weed with which our garden is overrun, whence has it come, and why?

The answer is simple, and like so much that is simple it is the more confusing. This weed, to continue the metaphor, is not the product of an accident, its growth is not due to the unforeseen intervention of some 'evil spirit' which has done us injury in spite of all our good intentions. It will be well for our safety and moral integrity if we assume full responsibility for it from the start. The gardener sowed the seed, and furthermore the gardener is each one of us. The gardener who is responsible for this crop of undesirable consequence is still active in ourselves at the present time. It is active in our parsons and our teachers, in our churches and our schools, in our law courts and our banks, in our business offices and our political leaders. As it has been in the past in those generations who have brought us up, so it is in the present in ourselves. War is gathered where war is sown, and those who have been unwittingly responsible are many. Amongst them (last but not least) our own present selves are not to be forgotten.

For this is the heart of the problem. Our trouble does not lie with those of evil genius who would injure us, but with those of good intention who would alter us, fixing upon convenient moral principles which seem to them to be the best for us. The problem of our lives would be so much easier if there were indeed some Evil One who could be thus cast out and punished for the evil motive which possessed him to interfere with us. The trouble, however, is all the other way, for the evil consequences are sown not by evil but by good intentions. This problem is so deeply rooted and so active in its unrest, because when the seed was sown it always seemed to be the seed of peace, which paradoxically changed its nature in the soil to produce this overwhelming crop of war.

Even in our search for peace there are so many of us who do not help to ease the strain of misunderstanding. They are the ones who would, with reasonable gesture and excellent intention, either eliminate the problem altogether or eliminate the one whom they think threatens to be the aggressor. But how can such aggressiveness ever cure aggressiveness? It seems easy now to be wise so long after the event, but the idea that the Great War was a war to end war was surely one of the simplest fallacies for which human foolishness and false hopes ever fell. How can war end war, or intolerance be made to cure intolerance? It is upon the advice of this fallacious sentiment, however, that the seed of war was and is still being sown, by those who would aggressively interfere with reality, rather than keep a watchful and friendly eye upon those differences which present themselves in the occasional form of enemies across our frontiers.

It is this simple habit of assuming in our own minds the divine authority of omniscient power and right to choose for others that has led us to the present condition of established impotence. Thus paradox thrusts the unwary into that perdition from which his every effort was to escape. Those who must-have peace, because they are afraid of reality, by their aggressiveness sow further seeds until they must-have war.

The seed of this most fruitful harvest of our times is to be found in ourselves and in our mode of thought. It is established, as deeply rooted as our heart's attitude towards life. Seeing that this weed is so firm within ourselves, surely it should be plain that it is no use to declare war upon our neighbours, thus hoping the better to ensure our peace. This conflict is at home within ourselves, and its solution must always be found solely within ourselves; not by external interference, nor by moralizing with missionary sentiment for the advantage of some other poor misguided fellow creature, but by a process of progressive insight, with the hand of action stayed lest we interfere even with the reality of ourselves. It may be a strain that we should thus accept essential difference; but, when it decides to eliminate that which is not as good as it might be for us, we must temper the swiftness of that quick moral judgment which seems so surely right.

Inward Conflict

Life is conflict. This problem of the external conflict in our lives is a projection from within ourselves of the bilateral mechanism from which life itself is developed. The habit of fixation is a consequence of an attitude which prefers unrelated absolutes. Thus there always seems to be a greater measure of safety to be found in some good but unrelated 'it', standing alone and fixed; but life depends upon movements of relationships, where there is difference between one and the other. History is but a projection upon the wall of life of this inward pattern of our own mind. Since then I am that error which seems to me to be outside myself, how can I rule it out, without at the same time applying the knife of such surgical elimination to the deep roots of my own heart?

It may seem a platitude thus to stress the fundamental problem of the mind which is divided against itself, but it raises the question—If this mind is thus divided so deeply against itself, then should it be, or should it not? Should the division be urgently bridged and the conflict thus eliminated, so that our minds are made one; or is there some other method by which the duality of self may be tolerated, recognizing that it is the law of life for it to be thus, and therefore that it is not to be altered by our sense of egotistical self-importance? Am I one or two? If I am two, ought there to be this difference within myself? If I could solve that problem, I might then be better able to deal with my different neighbours, who are also different from me.

The problem of war is the fundamental problem of life itself. It is the problem of conflict, relationships and movement. Therefore there can be no satisfactory approach to it which does not itself contain the full scope of life. The tools which we use for our study and research must be plastic enough, subtle enough, to weigh and measure the very sources of life, its forms, meanings and manifestations. There is a heavy responsibility upon any technique which is prepared to state that it is able to deal surely with the problem of life. The technique should be that of Psychology, but it is to be doubted whether there is any one psychology which is big enough to deal adequately with this problem. The system must be very large that is to include within its scope the ways of living things and do them justice. Therefore some liberty must be allowed to make use of such ideas as seem suitable, to go far afield if necessary, and occasionally to make statements of ridiculous simplicity. Life is like that, and there is nothing more surprising to the students of these vital phenomena than the discovery that it is always the simplest matters about which we are most ignorant. We can be fairly sure that the common words of four letters and less all refer to matters which we do not understand. Peace has five letters and war but three, but neither of these words is easily confined within any system of understanding.

The Self-Important Self

We find it very difficult to keep our sense of perspective and proportion in regard to the importance of ourselves. This is not really to be wondered at, because it is one of the fundamental disadvantages of our essential individuality that we should feel ourselves so keenly different, and so supremely important. I AM; and therefore it is extremely difficult for me to realize that for yourself you are as I am to me. It is impossible for one person to feel how it feels to be another. If we could estimate quantitatively in regard to the measure of this self-importance, the value of I AM would be very high indeed, and the value of any YOU that I AM NOT would be relatively very low. This sense of self-importance has the effect of colouring many of our values, both in space and time. It is hard for us to realize that the place where we spent our summer holiday a short time ago still continues even though we are not there. Peace 'in our time' and for ourselves, is all we ask.

At the breakfast table we may read of earthquakes in Japan, of tornadoes in America, of tragedy and sudden death, but they are less stimulating to us than the sugar in our coffee, because we are not there. Whether in space or time, the same exaggerated importance is attached to ME. For HIM the important pages of history began with his birth, or by a gratuitous extension, with A.D. 1. His family is an extension of himself and therefore only slightly less important, and his country is the same. There have never been any problems apart from the ones upon which he is engaged, and it is sad news indeed for philosophers to be told that there is no question that has not already been not only asked but also often answered, although it seems so urgently necessary that we should tell the world the truth today.

For him, religion began with Christianity—there could not and should not be any other. Because there is only this one self that is ME, therefore there can be only one country, to be supported because it never could be wrong. It is awkward for his self-assurance

45

that political parties should be divided into opposites, but he has not the slightest doubt that his party is the only one which is possessed of common sense, sympathy and every other virtue. When it comes to questions of colour, that which he adorns is the only one, and the inferiority of yellow, black or red is simply beyond question. No self-respecting Englishman could doubt that his country, his colour and his religion are not the only ones that are eventually best for the rest of the world. Notice that not only is it right for him, but also for the whole world, that they should come within his limited perspective and egocentric colour scheme.

Perhaps this picture of the self-important self may have been slightly overdrawn, but the problem of perspective is very near the heart of our question. We see our own projected image upon the wall of life and it is so obvious that it is the only one. There is no room for any other in our space or time, we are so sure that there ought to be but one, and which one that should be it is not difficult for us to say, because we can see nothing beyond this projected primacy of ourself. Of course the lion ought to lie down with the lamb; but according to which is ME we shall decide which one is to be inside the other.

Genesis

But let us see; and since one beginning is probably as good as another, we may take for our beginning the story of Genesis, which deals with the Garden of Eden and what happened there. We learn that one was made into two, from which much trouble followed. From this event of separation, by which a border-line that was impassible was placed between the male and female, there was born not only life, but also pain and effort. That space which divided them was the birth of disappointment. Unity became dual and multiple, peace became war, and laughter was dissolved in tears. When faced with the reward of their impatient curiosity, it may be assumed that both Adam and Eve felt that it would be better if they could get back to that state of simple unity from which they had sprung. 'We were as one, but now we are divided; we were at peace, but now we are at war; let us go back then, for surely we ought to be at peace, as one, again.'

In this legend of a cosmic as well as individual Genesis, there is symbolized the simple fact of all our own experience, for we also have been separated from that Paradise within the mother's timeless womb, in which we once were one. There was a time when child and mother were as one, but unity and security were shattered by the pain of separation, and agony was expressed inadequately in the child's first cry. That umbilical cord, which was the symbol of our unity, has since been cut, not once but many times, as we have been separated during the course of our development from that maternal and domestic circle, which was at various times the source of birth, food, feeling and thinking. It seems as if we can but change one umbilical cord for another, as we move through these extensions of experience, at the price of the pain of a new weaning. We long to be attached again to breast or bottle, but even when we are deprived of that comforting privilege, we are still given the freedom of some

47

maternal protection, as upon her expansive lap we lie relaxed and enjoy this sense of intimate contact and unity. Alas, the period of our rest is not for long, because it seems as if some inexorable force is continually urging this wanderer farther and farther from the garden from which he was first separated at birth. There is no permanent resting place for him, until finally even the protective shell of thoughtfulness within which he was nurtured in the nursery becomes shattered by contact with the vital world, and the last of his more intimate links with mother has been severed.

There ensues a period of wandering, until some other attachment is made, some new cord forged of greater or lesser subtlety attaching him to creed or dogma, hope or faith, individual or cause, as mother-substitute. Will this one last; can this be fixed? Or is hope once again to prove false, with the repeated experience of lost love? The important thing to observe, however, in this process of our life's development through failing hopes, is the rhythmic regularity with which appetite is gratified only to be followed subsequently by hunger. Having is intermittent with losing, and pain hard upon the heels of fleeting pleasure. This is the deepest root of the rhythm of life which is always pursuing us with alternating light and shadow, waking and sleeping, rest and effort, giving and taking, in constant circulation between the two poles of which our vital existence is composed. This duality is the source of all our painful paradox. If we pursue the desired objective by the direct method, and if having gained it we try to fix it, we find we are eventually defeated by the law of life, which depends upon a more intermittent rhythm than that of 'what I have I hold'. Our straight lines bend to flowing curves, and our cherished fixed points are swept away in time.

Seen and unseen, the duality is always there, although we are in many ways unwilling to recognize the reality of the unseen. We moralize, as if we ought not to believe in it, because it is unseen. For instance, because it has not been possible to 'prove' the existence of the spirit, Science rejects the hypothesis of incarnation (spirit in matter). However, if convenient, it is a hypothesis which science should not refuse on moral grounds, because science itself is dependent upon many such metaphysical conveniences for all its most satisfactory superstructure. Incarnation is a hypothesis which is simple, and which well accords with our experience of duality in other ways. It is possessed of historical importance, as in one form or another it has never left the stage of metaphysics. It is not unreasonable to suppose that within the form there is that which animates it. This is merely another example of the universal duality, light within lantern, I within Me, and spirit within the flesh of body-mind. We may not like this dualistic conception of life, but let us be warned that if at this point we adopt a concept of convenient unity, we may become involved in all those fallacies which follow upon such anxious misunderstanding. If there are two then for Heaven's sake let there be two, because if one aspect of reality is constantly ignored and yet is alive and part of our experience, not only is it beyond our control, but it is also made our enemy. Since we have threatened to destroy it, it will seem to threaten us. If this unseen enemy is the Spirit of our lives, then we are indeed paying a heavy price for a metaphysical misunderstanding, based upon indignant moral self-righteousness in the name of Science.

Always there are these two related poles which, through their relationship, cause the flow of life. Yet always, each of these two regards the other one with suspicion upon the plane of human relationships. In the home there is no hesitation in the mind of parents that the children ought to be like them. It is a little suspicious that in the minds of the children a similar fallacy also takes place, 'We ought to be one.' On both sides there is this fundamental agreement—'Yes, we ought to be one'. Yes, but which one? That is the argument which is the source of so much subsequent misunderstanding in the world. We may be agreed that we ought to be one, but which of us is to be so conveniently eliminated in the process of unification? Stated in a simple way it sounds perhaps too simple, yet it seems to be the very root of the whole problem of war. Since there are these two, which one are we to choose? Sheep or goats, wheat or chaff, self or other? Or—is it possible—both?

Since we have started by this reference to the story of Genesis, we will continue to take it as the myth for our convenient interpretation of life's problem. It is interesting to see how the duality is expressed in the story: 'In the beginning God created the heaven and the earth.' From darkness we are told that he created light, and from the water, earth. (We may learn therefore, that darkness is not so bad a thing after all, and that water is not only for drinking and washing.) 'The spirit of God moved, and created the space in the midst of the waters, dividing the waters from the waters.' 'A river went out of Eden to water the garden and from thence it was parted and became four heads.'

All was well until Adam and Eve felt guilty after eating of the fruit of the Tree of Knowledge of good and evil, on the advice of the 'serpent'. With this birth of guilt we shall be dealing in a subsequent chapter, using the same analogy from the Book of Genesis, but it is sufficient for us at the moment to draw this conclusion: where there are two, there are potential enemies. The question is, however, whether this situation of potential enmity is such a bad thing. But first we must consider further the distinction between 'opposites' and 'contraries.'

Yang and Yin

It is curious that, under the influence of Christianity, we seem to have become increasingly sure of the disadvantages of duality during the last two thousand years. Both science and logic, as well as religion, are more inclined today to adopt a policy of elimination under the sword of moral judgment. If this is 'good', then up and up and up; but if it is 'bad', then let it be cast into outer darkness, which is a very bad place. For science, darkness or ignorance is evil; for logic, chaos is evil and for religion (in the guise of Christianity), Satan the adversary is an evil force, which does not represent the will of God, other than as an opportunity to show His supremacy by casting Satan out. The dragon of St. George is another aspect of this Prince of Darkness, adversary of all our more saintly hopes, and our patriotic deference to the saintly technique is shown by the way in which we teach it in our schools as the way for our children to follow. Wherever we find evil, it is to be actively pursued and eliminated, and this process is backed with so much moral fervour that it is very rarely criticized. It is assumed to be the only way, as if evil is a bad thing and there is no more to be said.

As a matter of fact there is a great deal more to be said, and it has all been said during the course of the three thousand years which preceded the advent of Christianity and our present era of unrest. Our Western science and philosophy have only of recent years discovered the metaphysic of the four-dimensional system, and yet it seems safe to say that, thousands of years ago, this metaphysic was acted upon in the religious and philosophic systems of China and Persia, India and Egypt with far greater accuracy than it is today. It is not new to the New or Old Testament, but it seems to have been lost from the teaching of Christ in the process of the organization of the Christian Church.

The basic couple in the old teaching were the primordial principles of Darkness and Light. These were called Yang and Yin, and were regarded as positive and negative poles, but there was no question as to which of these two was to be the chosen one. They were both regarded as vessels of the indwelling spirit, dual manifestations of the inexpressible One, which were part of the necessary frame and formula within which the spirit moved and had its being. The dragon and the darkness were regarded, like the water, as the sources from which was born light; and all experience was appropriately referred to the fundamental symbolism of the roots, trunk and branches of the Tree of Life. The roots dwelt in the darkness, the harvest in the light. Nothing was wrong in itself; but it might be wrongly used, misused in space or time and thus become obscene.

It seems curious that the policy of the last two thousand years (which was never essentially the teaching of Christ, although it seems to have been regarded as such by the Christian Church) should have been so misguided as to preach a technique of eliminating 'evil' roots in order the better to obtain the 'good' fruit. In fact it looks as if the Church itself has fallen into the error of eating prematurely of the forbidden fruit of the tree of knowledge of good and evil; judging so swiftly, it has assumed the good and eradicated the evil and the adversary. Such policy in practice must surely be unwise. Morally it is but another form of anxious egotism, stealing fruits before they are ripe, in case someone else may get them first. Farmers, and others who are wise in the practice of life, realize that there is nothing wrong with manure, as long as it is in the right place, at the root, hidden beneath the soil. Under other less suitable circumstances it may well be judged obscene, but that is only an error of misplacement or a false relationship. Those who study truth realize that there is no such thing as 'absolute' right or wrong, because there is no such thing as 'absolute' anything in a world in which the fundamental law is relative. Experience of any kind is the function of a relationship. It is derived from unseen antecedents, which act as parents of this consequent child.

VICIOUS CIRCLE

Yet we must persuade our minds against some difficulty that all these absolutes are erroneous judgments, and that only that which is relative is really true. In fact it is not that which is 'evil' which has defeated us, but rather that which has been fixed as if it were absolute 'good'. Such fallacious assumption, convenient as it may seem to fearful minds, must always run counter to the free-moving flow of life.

The same error of selectivity, up with this and down with that, has also been operating in regard to the value allotted to male and female. There has been no doubt in the minds of mankind that the female, being the less visibly efficient, was inferior to the male. This judgment has of recent years been made more obvious by the way in which the modern movement for equality of the sexes has forced women and men into open competition, thereby showing how much women envy the male his masculine superiority. Yet how can there be equality between any two opposite poles? If there were, all movement must cease; which is perhaps what anxiety is seeking, but it would be only a negative state of death, compared with which a more positive state of death would be infinitely preferable. (The words positive and negative thus applied to death show how meanings of the same word may still be poles apart. Thus if we speak of death, we well may ask, which death?) Selectivity in any form, or applied to any subject, is always trying to raise one aspect of the duality at the expense of the suppression of the other, and it is doubly unfortunate that this misunderstanding should be applied to women. They share the indignity, however, with the whole company of dragons and darkness, water and the spirit, intuition, sleep and death, besides such apparently unimportant 'negatives' as the unseen, space and ignorance. For whether they are regarded collectively or individually, these are all 'bad things', it seems, to be eliminated as suddenly as possible: until we are all one and the same, devitalized hermaphrodites possessing Heaven and possessed by fullest virtue, fixed in the eternal light of conscienciousness, living for ever—because such absolute perfection could then never be threatened by the error of unreasonable change.

Metaphysics, Science and Medicine

This method of moral selectivity leads to bad science as well as bad religion. Wherever it operates selectively, rejecting 'evil' or any other part of truth, the scientific method is to blame for its moral prejudice or religious bias. If the effect of science is to select or still, then as far as life is concerned it operates as aggressively as the murderer who kills. For life is movement; and whether in science or religion, these moral prejudices share the role of murderer when they are thus anxious to fix convenient absolutes so that they cannot move. Seeking for knowledge, we are assailed by paradox, because any increase of it must also be balanced by an increase in the horizon of our ignorance. Thus it cannot be good to know, for knowledge wrongly used, unbalanced, can be as unfriendly to us as the worst of our ignorance. However favourable the prospect, whenever a good idea is obeyed in absolute disregard for its relationships, then it has become only the evil half of paradox.

The method of hopeful efficiency which isolates objects in order the better to observe them under a microscope one at a time, although it may pass under the name of scientific accuracy, adding much to convenient knowledge, has been fatal to the progress of the more important aspects of the study of mankind. For the truth of the scientific method, it is important never to forget the limitations of the qualifying phrase 'in the circumstances'. 'In these circumstances' (which include all conditions of time and space, apparatus, sensorial and conscious mechanisms, the subjective bias of the observer, etc.) we can act as reporters of phenomena, but science cannot claim the right either to choose or to explain.

In particular, Medicine has taken too much upon itself, because it does not go far enough. Pseudo-scientific orthodoxy in medicine is based upon a false metaphysic of moral prejudice, to which life cannot give up its secret key. Firmly established upon only one bank of the River of Life, studying only material effects (pathology, pharmacology, physiology, etc.) in isolation, it selects its material evidence. But since it does not allow for the existence of the unseen other bank, it is without insight as to the causes of changes in living phenomena. Everything is seen superficially as if that were all, and then diagnosed in isolation.

It would not matter if the 'scientific' attitude in medicine would be content to act as a reporter, pursuing the way of empiricism to its logical limits. Instead, however, it introduces the age-old fallacies of moral theology, and proceeds to justify its findings by a process of systematic rationalization which often finds it hard to explain one hypothesis that does not work, by the addition of another that makes matters only more confused. The metaphysic of medicine is crowded with such hypotheses which have been tacked on to one another in order to take the place of the neglected reality of the unseen cause of life.

As doctors we have been trained to see 'effects'. This would not matter if we did not pretend also to see 'causes', for these are not really to be found on the surface-level of apparent phenomena, which we have been taught to regard as all that matters. Thus it is not to be wondered at that the 'science' of medicine has no knowledge of what is life, or what that power is which is manifested in so many different ways. There is no explanation of sleep (which is therefore waste of time), or of death (which is a bad thing to be avoided); faints and fits are undesirable phenomena to be treated and got rid of symptomatically; and colds and cancer fail to impress the examining physician with the real nature of the problem: What is Life?

In spite of the fact that the burden of its pseudo-scientific curriculum weighs with increasing force upon each successive generation of students, the art of Medicine gains nothing of insight into vital causes, because of its moralistic attitude of insisting that only that which is seen is real, and that the unseen has no right to exist. Yet Life is unseen, force is unseen, and all that seeing can reckon with is the manifestation of external effects, of which we can never hope to see the cause. Medicine, therefore, which bases itself upon so obscure a moral prejudice and misunderstanding of the scientific method as to abjure the intangible, must lose control of that very life which it is its function to save. We can see so

57

many effects and we can, for rational purposes perhaps, tell ourselves that we have seen a cause, but the
causes upon these planes of visible influence are very
superficial and require causes behind causes, until we
get lost in the infinite regress of what caused cause.

The truth is that we are sick; and it is no wonder
that we are sick of sickness, too. We may hope that,
amongst our many offers of external aid, Psychology
will help to restore stability and poise. And so it may:
but there are many psychologies, and all are not so
sound themselves that they can balance us. There is no
lasting solution to the pain and penalty of life by offering reasonable answers to endless anxious questions,
nor by repeated suggestion that seeks to buttress the
failing hope that all is well. Nor does a prolonged process of analysis that seeks first cause for blame in some
experience of frustration, whether at breast or womb or
elsewhere amongst the pains of life, go far enough. The
'unconscious' is not to be made 'conscious', nor all
mankind 'reasonable', before we may enter into the
Kingdom, as worthy citizens of life. Of knowledge and
advice, of hope and reason, of cause and blame, we
have already more than plenty. But of balance, discipline and illumination, there is still room for more.
If Psychology in its own or any other name, will teach
us to accept the truth about ourselves and others, seen
and unseen, yesterday but tomorrow also, it well may
prove by its use of common sense, good manners and
true good humour, to be the saviour of our times. But
first we must learn this paradox, that ills must be accepted before they can be healed.

It may seem surprising that so much of the pain and

penalty of our existence should be due to so small a matter as an error of metaphysics, but that is the case. There are always these two alternatives: morals or manners; you or me; is or ought; observation or action. The choice is vital, even though it may seem to be so much a matter of abstract metaphysics. If we can learn to live within the discipline of this conjunction 'and', then the matter of our relationships can still be at peace; but if we adopt this attitude of moral prejudice which insists upon a selection between you or me, by which the wrong must be eliminated, then we are involved in conflict, for 'ought' means WAR.

The pattern of life is cruciform and circular, and so requires the four-dimensional metaphysic of the double duality, based upon polar relationship. The scientific method, in medicine, education and religion, if it is to be properly applied, is the method of unconditional illumination. The truth is found, not by elimination of the undesirable, but by a fuller vision which allows for the supremacy of the unseen. In this matter, the scientific method may also serve the cause of Peace.

The Privilege of Choice

In order to safeguard ourselves against the possibility of this self-important self becoming unduly prejudiced in its own favour, we should be wise to make plain the possible alternatives in regard to this decisive matter of our right to choose. Have we the right to choose or not, and is our much invoked and often praised free-will to be the cherished guarantor of our endeavour? It seems to have been decided for us long ago that we have this right to choose between what we like and dislike. Even beyond that, it has been put upon us as a moral obligation that we should exercise the right of judgment as between This and That, saying that this is good and that is bad (therefore up with this good and down with that bad), with the added obligation that we should then act according to such choice. The courageous and praiseworthy duty of St. George was to eliminate the Dragon, and the Devil as evil Adversary was to be excommunicated with bell, book and candle. Thus the root of all 'evil' was to be eradicated; but before we are so sure as to the rights of such prejudicial behaviour, let us at least declare that there is another alternative for our due consideration. In place of such negative and aggressive rights and duties of elimination, there is the positive alternative of acceptance of all that is for our digestion at the feast of life, without picking and choosing according to our personal taste.

From the practical point of view we are called upon to decide whether we believe in absolute evil as something which can be eliminated or, on the other hand, whether we believe that evil and good are always associated twins, from which it is impossible to dissect the one without at the same time killing the other. Let us look at our own experience and see if we can thus deal eliminatively with the evil one. Do we believe in punitively ridding ourselves of the one who has been proved mistaken, or in lovingly including him as the Prodigal Son? Do we believe in punishing enemies or in loving them? Do we believe that our greatest danger is to be found wherever there exists our greatest asset, and that fall follows rising pride; or do we believe that it is possible to go up and up and up for ever, without soon losing contact with reality? Do we believe in the absolute unity of good, opposed in deadly battle to the absolute unity of evil, so that we can safely back the one to win against the utter elimination of the other; or do we believe that life without either of these protagonists would be worse than dead? Is truth single, or is it paradox? Is there some Heaven for our fixed achievement, distant or only round the next corner; or is it here now, earned by our attitude towards accepted Hell? Is there a state of peace in safety, or is there only peace about a state of uncertain and potential war?

The problem may be regarded as very metaphysical or theological, but it is the problem of life, which in one way or another we decide according to the way of our behaviour. This is the fundamental problem of peace and war: Should there be conflict and, if so, what is our attitude towards it to be? Is peace to be achieved by eliminating war; or is peace, on the other hand, to be achieved through the acceptance of the polarity of conflict?

The problem is peculiarly one of East and West, in that the West has for long identified itself with the moral obligation of choice and with the concept of free-will. Eastern philosophers, on the other hand, have declared for a more humble attitude, regarding free-will as a vainglorious illusion on the path of unlicensed egotism. The result of these two attitudes towards life may seem to prove up to now the advantages of the Western method of effort, purpose and ambition. What we have to consider, however, is the disadvantage which may coexist with the advantage that belongs to the

61

Western method. The East is sleepy and the West aggressively determined; can we choose the one or the other, or are we again to decide to accept both? The symbolism of ancient China was built upon the fundamental differentiation of matter into Yang and Yin, which stood for darkness and light, female and male, respectively. From this basic duality, all subsequent dualities were regarded as developing by a process of splitting one into two, one into two, one into two, on the general principle that there was a black and white aspect to everything, and that everything could be divided into seen and unseen, or male and female aspects. The dragon in this symbolism stood for darkness (out of which was created light) and for female (eternally virgin, out of whom was created the male). It should give us cause to think and wonder whether the attitude of the last two thousand years has been so fundamentally an improvement upon that of five thousand years ago. It looks as if one gain has been paralleled by another loss, so that what we have gained on the swings we have lost on the roundabouts. The last two thousand years have added greatly to our discriminative ability and to the accumulation of our knowledge, but with the additions which have occurred we have lost more and more the power to control the forces to which we have given birth. So much of life has been lost even since the Middle Ages, when language was more living than it is at the present day, and men were living closer to the earth and God. It is as if the dictionary, whilst adding to our vocabulary, has had the effect of pinning down these verbal butterflies and robbing them of life.

DIAGRAMS

The dilemma is universal and occurs on every hand, because the problem with which we are dealing is that of related effects, the cause of which lies deep behind the mirrors of experience in the unseen beyond. If this unseen beyond is to be eliminated as evil, cursed as darkness, and excommunicated as the undesirable adversary, then what is to become of life? The answer to this question seems to be precisely that which has happened in our present state: namely, a crisis in which forces have become increasingly out of hand, because of our ignorance and unwillingness to learn the laws which would control them. Wherever we look the problem is the same, and there can be no solution of the state of our personal and social unrest until our manners have adopted a more tolerant attitude towards the difference between these separated but related parts.

Diagrams

In concluding this chapter, we may illustrate the points which have been raised by reference to some simple diagrams, because they make the argument more clear.

Diagram 2, 'Poles apart', illustrates (a) the general relationship of self and circumstances, female and male, nucleus and protoplasm, or any other duality, by two circles one within the other, A and B, related as positive and negative, Yang and Yin. The arrangement of the arrows indicates (b) the positive phase, where $A > B$, (c) the negative phase where $B > A$ and (d) the existence of conflict, where A and B are not reciprocal, but antagonistic (i.e. not only opposite, but also contrary).

DIAGRAM 2

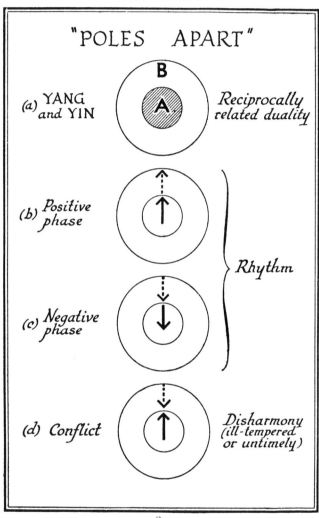

"POLES APART"

(a) YANG and YIN — Reciprocally related duality

(b) Positive phase

(c) Negative phase

Rhythm

(d) Conflict — Disharmony (ill-tempered or untimely)

DIAGRAM 3

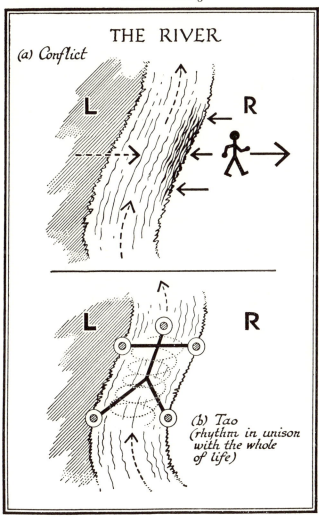

THE RIVER

(a) Conflict

L   R

(b) Tao
(rhythm in unison
with the whole
of life)

VICIOUS CIRCLE

Diagram 3, 'The River', carries the problem a stage further. The river has left bank and right. The left is lower, primitive, dark, the jungle, populated by 'denizens of the deep': the right is superior, civilized, light, organized in terms of knowledge and social convention. The right bank is 'better' and the left is 'worse'.

The upper half of the diagram illustrates the method of moral selection. We go up and up and up, with the related fear of the evil effect of going down, down, down. The little man is sure which way to go; up and on, progress and uplift, but he must build an impassible barrier to prevent himself from being attacked by the enemy on the other side of the river, and he must fix his advantages as best he can.

The lower half of the diagram tells another story. The little man has a foot in both worlds, and a hand in both worlds, for he has two hands and two feet. He is in a state of suspense between known and unknown, male and female, bridging the gap between two related poles, of which he is the mediator. He is living on a bridge, but he is in unison with life and has no other enemy than that which is beloved. He is what the Chinese describe as 'in Tao', experiencing the wholeness of life. He is a man of peace about this conflict, he is a holy, whole, and healthy man.

In Diagram 4, we see the 'All-round man', related to these two worlds of poles apart, divided against himself, but capable of unity within himself, and also in regard to his surrounding circumstances. Perhaps the biggest error that we can ever make, is the one by which we have learnt to regard the 'self' as expressed in the superficial pattern of our arms and legs,

66

DIAGRAM 4

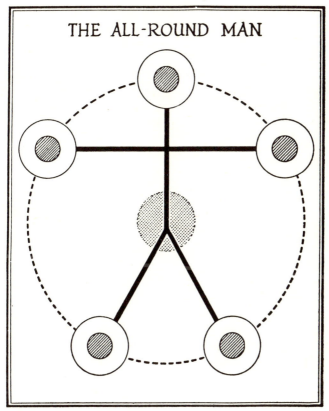

THE ALL-ROUND MAN

body and head. This diagram may serve to remind us that a truer pattern of the self is spherical, containing unseen centre, upon the surface of which are distributed all those sense organs with which in turn we 'see' the world of our experience. Thus the superficial self has the double function both of orifice to digest incoming information, and also of these active limbs with which we move across the stage of our experience. All incoming sensorial impressions are thus referred to some level of the spinal cord, from which again emanate those motor impulses which are responsible for action. The rhythmic law of interchange—outside, inside, outside—sensorial, motor, sensorial—rest, movement, rest —seems to act in constant repetition, linked with the deeper rhythm of life itself upon which we so uncertainly depend. If either of these two aspects of our experience is eliminated, we are either blind or paralysed; and this seems to be what indeed has happened, to place us in the awkward situation in which we find our present civilization.

In Diagram 5, 'Denizens of the Deep', we see the Tree of Life planted with its roots in the unseen, from which it draws its energy for being and becoming. A transverse line divides Light from Darkness, Yin from Yang, earth from water, male from female, tree from roots, and the animals we like above the surface from those beneath to which we feel a natural abhorrence, such as snakes, worms and sea-serpents, spiders, mice and rats. Reference to these latter shows how deeply rooted is our natural and instinctive prejudice against these denizens of the unseen, and experience in dreams (illustrative of patients' problems) bears out anew the necessity for coming to terms with these our apparent enemies, and making friends of them. At the right-hand side of the picture, repeated from Diagram 3, the figure of a man is shown, represented in both worlds. The polar opposition is there represented of heart and head, and the organism of self is illustrated in terms of the

DIAGRAM 5

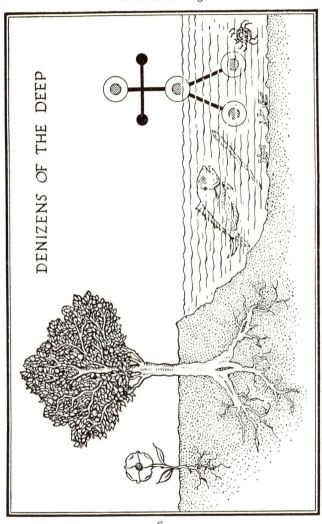

DENIZENS OF THE DEEP

familiar pattern of a small circle within another, nucleus within protoplasm, unseen hidden within seen.

Our last picture (Diagram 6) may go further than the others to illustrate the solution of this problem upon which we are engaged, but nevertheless it will raise as many problems as those to which it suggests some fair conclusion. It is an illustration of stimulus and response, and raises the question—when this happens, what should we do? Although the picture represents the symbolic relationship of a flower and a bee, for our more personal interest it may be taken to be the bald head of a man who wishes to be allowed to sleep, and finds his rest interfered with by the intermittent buzzing of a mosquito. Here is an annoying stimulus, threatening to break the peace of sleeping majesty. Polarity is defined: mosquito and Bald Head; snore-snore, Buzz-Buzz.

There is a strong probability that Bald Head will be irritated beyond bearing, so that he will rise to eliminate, if he can, the mosquito. For him we may assume an easy victory, and for the mosquito an untimely end. But such premature success for adventurous aggressiveness will only lead our bald-headed friend who wants to sleep, a step farther into the deepening bog of successful warfare, for there is always another mosquito to occupy the place of the fallen one. The time will come when he meets some kind of enemy who cannot thus be eliminated, and finally he must learn that there is another way, which is a path of non-resistance. He must learn to sleep 'despite' and not 'because'; as he must learn also to live and to love, to understand and to heal, 'despite' and not 'because'.

DIAGRAM 6

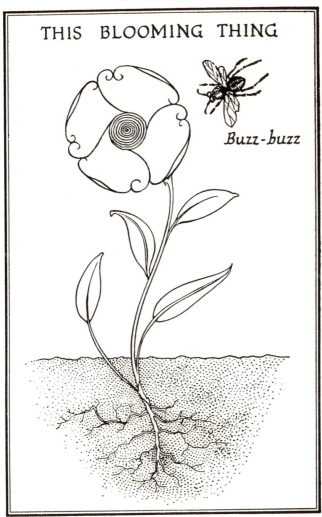

THIS BLOOMING THING

Buzz-buzz

VICIOUS CIRCLE

Life presents itself frequently with the persistent irritation of the mosquito to our would-be sleeper, and it is well for us to learn in the beginning this other way which does not seek immediately to eliminate the aggressive stimulus, but on the other hand is willing to accept it. The frequency of negative stimuli is endless; we cannot afford always to be so restless about them. (Is that what has happened to our over-active world: is it just being active about action?) We may give to this stimulus the significance of the negative, and we shall be right in also giving that same negative significance to the behaviour of the bald-headed aggressor, who would thus destroy his enemy. But is it possible to receive negative experience (i.e. pain) without adopting a negative attitude towards it (i.e. strain)? Can we develop a mental habit of relaxation about life, accepting what we dislike with the same spirit as that which we adopt towards what we like? Thus enemies are loved as friends are loved, although the enemy is disliked and the friend liked. (The fact that we love him does not mean that he is any less the enemy for that.)

These two alternative methods may be illustrated by the idea of a flower which closes like a fist to keep out the offender, shutting itself against everything which it dislikes; and on the other hand by the flower which remains as open as a friendly hand in the face of all experience, whatever it may be. There are those of us who, trying with strained effort to shut out or eliminate all that we do not like, and adding moral prejudice to the judicial egotism of our acclaimed free-will, will find it difficult to adopt this other method, but it is not hard to see the possibility that it provides for peace. It is amongst those who can behave thus as men of good-will, observantly tolerant, wise and balanced, that we hope to find our friends. They seem to have found the better answer to the pressing question: 'What should we do with this blooming thing?'

It looks as if our time is going widdershins, the wrong way round the sun. Our civilization is in a whirl, but backwards: movement is rapid, but threatens to be in the direction of decline and fall: we are caught in a vicious circle, from which we cry: 'Let me out: give me peace!' How did we get into this vice? If we could answer that question we should have more guarantee that our freedom would not be again misused, if we had another chance. It is no use to try to build our house again, if there is the same error as before in our yard-stick and set-square.

It seems as if what we now need to learn has some-thing to do with method, rather than with the know-ledge that method may apply. We have the knowledge, but do not know how to use it. It is because our method has been wrong that we have failed. In all matters of life, the direct method is a failure, pregnant with dis-aster. It never pays to move by direct attack, striving aggressively to achieve the desired objective. The good is not gained by trying to lose the bad; happiness is not discovered by pursuit of it; children are not made good by eliminating evil from their midst; enemies are not made friends by chastizing them; sinners are not saved by blaming them; nor are the sick healed by the simple process of cutting out disease.

The effect of all such partial pursuit of that which seems so 'good', is that we are in turn pursued into

73

persecution by 'evil'. Knowledge is pursued by ignorance, power by the threat of impotence, wealth by poverty, and saints by the fear of sin. All race miserably round and round the ragged rocks of despair, but widdershins. It is indeed hopeless that way; yet not altogether hopeless if we would employ another method more allied to life.

For life is relative, not absolute, and requires the indirect method of due parentage in time. The mind which thinks in terms of single cause (e.g. 'I did it', or 'if only . . .' or 'because . . .') is thinking wrongly, for the only single cause is God, which is beside the point. We are many, not one, indirectly linked and multiplied in complex relationships. The direct method is a fallacy, which puts us wrong with life, and gives us precipitate movement in a false direction. But it seems so simple, because it makes direct appeal to efficiency and all that consciousness holds dear.

Peace is not to be pursued by any means aggressively, but gently wooed, which implies the indirect method. Above all, the method requires complete honesty, both of purpose and of payment where price is due. Peace may be a phantasy for our escape: or it may be a fact of living growth. Which is it to be? The direct method pursues the former phantasy. The fact remains, for humbler wooing in spite of all uncertainty.

CHAPTER II: ANXIETY

SUMMARY

Dreams.

Progress and Evolution. Movement is a function of relationship; rhythm; balanced curves.

Suspense. Is true but anxiety would fix.

Anxiety. Definitions; strain about strain; the importance of an attitude; fear and panic.

Reality of Metaphysics. Some examples; relativity and purpose; the fallacy of free-will.

Fear. Definitions; desirable or undesirable.

Thinking. What it can do about anxiety; two modes of thought; the plain man's limitations.

Feeling and Emotion. Definitions; the importance of analysis; debit and credit; the holding of the bridge; emotion means aggressiveness.

Nerves. Diseased physicians; the defensive negative; hypersensitiveness and hyperactivity; metaphysical, not material, error.

Tolerant Sensitiveness. The error of identification; the meaning of suffering.

Self-Expression. Incarnation of 'spirit' in 'body-mind'; I in Me. Aladdin and the lamp; keep the Geni in the bottle.

Religion. The solvent of anxiety; fallacy and fact.

75

CHAPTER II: ANXIETY
DREAMS[1]

III. 'The Time-Track'

I was in a most beautiful field in radiant sunlight, in which the grass looked particularly lush and green and everything most pleasant. Playing carelessly in the field were half a dozen very happy-looking black kids (i.e. baby goats). By the side of the field, separated from it by a hedge, there ran a railway track. I was horrified to see one of the kids escaping from the field by crossing the track, and all the others followed him. I felt responsible and wondered how on earth I could get them back. Picking my way over the electrified rail, I managed to catch one of the kids and carry him under my arm into the field again, the others dutifully following, I was pleased to see.

Then the dream changed. I was in a shop buying an alarm clock. The man told me he had only got one, which was quite unique because it could be reversed, as the back contained a very useful workbasket. It had a large face, a garish orange colour, which I did not like, but I bought it because it was the only one.

IV. 'Snakes'

I found I had a snake somewhere round my neck, wriggling up under my chin, and I thought it was doing no good there, as it was altogether too high.

Then I saw that I had another one round me, about waist-high, and I knew that it was better there.

[1] For comment, see Appendix (page 305-6).

Chapter II

ANXIETY

Progress and Evolution

Expressed as a function of relationship, life moves. Things are not so concrete or solid in their reality as they seem to be, because they thus depend upon their antecedent circumstances. The process of our thought makes reality seem to be more fixed than in fact it is; and unfortunately for us, we try to make reality fit our thoughtful sense of it, instead of more humbly seeing that our senses and thoughts should follow what in fact is true.

Feeling so sure of what is good for us, we try to fix the world in which we live, forcing it to fit straight lines, where life prefers the current curves of reciprocity and rhythm. We build as if time must not change; and argue within our conscious systems, devising a morality to support what life in its movement seems more willing to destroy. If there can be no progress, we glibly say, then what can be the meaning of life for us? Of course we must progress; up and up and up, on and on and on, good better best, never let it rest!

But life seems to move upon another plan; up-down-up-down; having-losing-having-losing; in-out-in-out;

77

seen-unseen-seen-unseen. Our insistence upon progress is liable to run contrary to life's larger law of
Evolution, which history can prove, however, to our
egotistic undoing. Neglected by us or not, the larger
law holds good; life moves both up and down, by day
and night, or life and death. The most upon which our
hopeful desire for Purpose and Progress can rely is a
spiral, returning whence it came, perhaps a little farther on, upon a different level of the scale of Evolution.
Even so it is better not to hope for much; the memory
of life is long and its time distances cause our brief span
of years to appear a little ridiculous, except to the urgent anxieties of self-righteous egotism. We may have
long to wait before we can be sure of progress. A lapse
of two thousand years is not very much in cosmic time,
and may well be spent on a negative phase of Evolution, returning to that centre from which an absolving
death leads to some new flowering of rebirth.

The gains of the past century have been in terms of
differentiated knowledge and of opportunity for effective action; now we can have and do so much more
than we could then. But is that all we mean by progress, or are we still in fact far behind that worth of
'being' which can appreciate or control this vast addition to our opportunities? The means to live are with
us now in plenty. We have a wealth of knowledge,
material abundance, but they seem only to provide
an oppressive burden of responsibility upon the heavy
heads of mankind, who are not yet ready to profit by
this surfeit of opportunity. In fact, we are in danger of
dying from this excess of Good Things. Our stomach
is too small, and we seem sick, staggering beneath the

burden, desiring still more, yet quite unable to assimilate even that which we have.

We are suffering the threat of an extinction, because we are not balanced. We have so much, and don't know what to do about it; nor have we yet discovered the law that 'Being' is despite our opportunities, not because of them. I AM is the deepest possible statement of the law of life; yet having and doing so much, how can I expect to find the space and time to BE? Progress is being called to account, Debit to balance Credit. The bargain of Mephistopheles and Faust remains, and we must pay our Soul in debt for these fine privileges of material progress. This is no angry voice from Heaven, no punishment from an impatient angry God. It is the law of Evolution, the rhythm of life, the inescapable amend, in regard to which it may indeed be said 'The wages of sin is death'.

Children of our past, we are reaping the seed of War so generously sown. Swiftly up means swiftly down, unless we can learn to lose even more swiftly than the law demands. It is no use asking or crying now for peace. The milk is spilt, the damage done, the seed is sown. How then are we to live and make amends in time?

First let us see, and then to understand. It is not enough merely to escape from our anxiety by too urgently doing something about it, for aggressiveness can be no cure for previous aggressiveness, nor can a negative get rid of any other negative. See, accept, suffer; this must be the way of the transgressor, until he has picked up the path again, in harmony of tune and time with life.

DIAGRAM 7

EVOLUTION

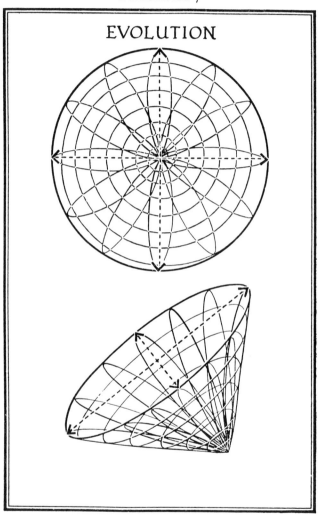

PROGRESS AND EVOLUTION

I AM: the simplest pattern of this state of being may be drawn as the flower or Mandala, significant of life (Diagram 7, page 80). The first diagram shows the 'flower' or energy system seen from above, the second from the side. Each shows the rhythm of spreading extension balanced by a central return; the relationship of a centre and circumference, each exercising a pull in turn, so-called Progress being followed by the alternating phase of Regress, or return being prior to another birth in moving time. We can well imagine how any egotist would object to such a law, wanting it otherwise to his secure advantage.

Upon the circumference of our circle of experience we manifest our differences, as the centre extends its parts by growth, from one to many, from egg to feathers, and from seed to leaves and flowers. In consciousness, the circumference contains the moving 'Now' of our experience; here is the learned knife of knowledge, and here is the opportunity for efficient exercise of active power.

The centre, on the other hand, represents the source from which all action is generated, and it is the deeper goal of our return. It is the source of our unity, the common stock of universal experience (hence the collective truth of intuition and 'common sense'). It is the phase in rhythm of sleep and death, of recreation and rebirth. This is the seed of our experience of deeper truths, through the paradox of the light which shines in this darkness, that is sometimes called 'mystical' because it is unseen and unexplained. Yet it always plays the most important part in every life, being the roots from which the tree must spring. It is the source of life itself, whether we are active or at rest, mystic or materialist.

In terms of polar difference, the circumference signifies action, distribution, masculinity, and is thus negative, or 'spending' energy. The centre signifies the resting, recreative, female phase, dark and unseen, and is thus positive, renewing energy. Awake, conscious, we spend energy upon the surface of our lives; asleep, and yet still ourselves, we earn our income from the unseen source of being. Between these two, we move in constant rhythm, always in both worlds and always in suspense. But consciousness thinks otherwise and plans its hopes accordingly.

Suspense

If this is true, since no one likes so great suspense, it is easily understood that we should believe the contrary, striving to fix this state of flux to some more permanent security of privilege. The success of these our efforts History has proved, is proving still, and will continue to prove again, until we have learnt more positive acceptance to the contrary.

But suspense is hard to learn: for what would happen to us if we did not try to bend life's movement to our will? It seems as if every ambition, every sense of moral decency, in fact every human need, urges our action to achieve, as instantly as may be, the satisfaction of desire. There is always the present tangle to be unravelled, the overwhelming mess to be cleared up, the threatening enemy at our very gates. Surely we must do something about that?

Looking at facts, we see this urgent tendency of our

DIAGRAM 8

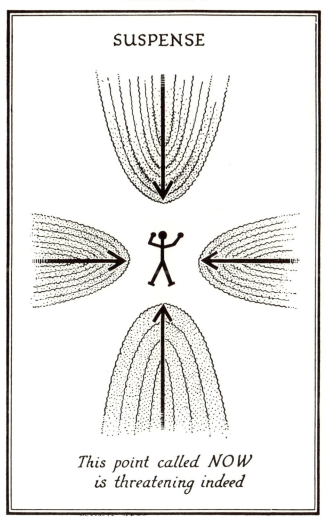

SUSPENSE

*This point called NOW
is threatening indeed*

moral compulsion and omnipresent obsession, acting as an aggressive dictator or regimental sergeant-major, issuing orders that seem to demand obedience. There are so many threats. Anxiety urges obedience, and we seem to be compelled to fall in with the other marching feet of the battalions of war.

But let us be still, and watch. To make it plainer for us to see and hesitate, Diagram 8 (page 83) shows the 'Little man' suspended between four moving worlds. Behind him is the Past, a little of it still to be seen amidst the falling mists of time. In front of him is the Future, shrouded, threatening. In his external world, within his ken and yet beyond his grasp, lurk enemies, seen and unseen, hopes deferred and questioning choice. Within, beneath his superficial exterior, there is a deeper self, hidden yet active, good and evil mixed, inextricably balanced. In his suspense, this point called NOW is threatening indeed, and justifies his sense of deep anxiety.

Anxiety

We may define anxiety as 'a state of strained desire or painful suspense'. It is noteworthy that this same definition would in fact fit life itself. In the previous chapter two different attitudes were discussed towards the basic duality of life, ('eliminated contrary' and 'accepted opposite') and illustrations were drawn from the Mandala or flower pattern. The basic law being one of related poles in a state of tension, more or less of strain, it was claimed that all experience is in some measure due to this polar relationship, and that we cannot truly conceive of anything existing 'absolutely'

84

by itself, in spite of conscious habit to the contrary. It seems to be a legitimate assumption on this hypothesis, therefore, to relate Spirit (unseen) and Matter (seen), as opposite poles of our system of experience, regarding Matter as the opposite of undifferentiated Spirit, Space as the opposite of its occupant, and Time as the other face of an opposed Eternity. Matter is thus Spirit in extension; and Spirit and Matter are actively related as poles apart, plus and minus, undifferentiated and differentiated, unseen and seen, darkness and light, female and male, Yang and Yin. Thus some degree of strain is of the order of life itself, and the question is, what we may hope to do about it.

Do we hope to eliminate it and, if so, by what means? Is it going to pay us in the end to get tense about tension and to strain against this sense of strain? Metaphysical, abstract, abstruse as our argument may at times appear, it is just at these times that the problem is one of most vital and everyday importance. Life is normally a situation of anxiety, in the sense that we cannot possibly know what is to happen to us in this moving world of discomfort and uncertainty. We can adopt the method of eliminative blindness and refuse to see the truth, or we can so dull our senses that they tell us nothing but those lies which we wish to believe. We can be negative in our fear of fear, adopting a policy of fixing flight instead of courage: 'I cannot bear the strain; let's not fear; let's not feel, but only sense, skin-deep; let's be surface, let's be certain, let's be safe.' We can thus choose, but if we do in any way attempt thus to beat the truth of time, aggressively, we shall thereby have joined the ministers of war.

ANXIETY

But if we are prepared to see life broad and balanced as it really is, we must recognize this state of inward strain. It is the experience of related parent and child, wife and husband, today and tomorrow. It is the experience of every moment of our lives, thus to be faced with uncertainty. If we join issue, becoming negative to that strain, then we have joined the legion of uncomfortable aggressors whose attitude towards life, being so restless about unrest, is in one way or another productive of that increased unrest which it is so unwilling to accept; seed of dis-ease, it is in general labelled with the loosely defined but opprobrious epithet, 'neurotic'. Identification with this alien enemy, or being negative about this negative, or strained about this strain, is so far to increase the undesirable condition as to create a larger measure of pain, which it was the ignorant purpose of this process to avoid.

It is now necessary to proceed with extreme care, in order to make quite clear the difference between Anxiety (a state of strain) and anxiety about anxiety (strain about strain). There is all the difference between these two states, yet there does not seem to be a word to make the distinction clear. If we may be allowed to use the word 'dimension', we could say that the latter is one dimension beyond the former. Then there is no reason why a dimension of Anxiety should not be carried any number of dimensions higher, to the nth power, e.g. by being anxious about being anxious about being anxious about being anxious. Many people have experienced this state, without being able in any way to describe their feelings in words. They would, however, be quite prepared to admit that there is all the difference in the world between anxiety and anxiety raised higher to the *n*th power.

It is perhaps curious to some that the nature of reality should be so abstract and metaphysical. The plain matter-of-fact man is quite content to assume that 'It is it' and 'That is that', and that if something is unseen it therefore *ipso facto* does not exist. To the careful observer, however, the truth is exactly opposite, because the more we go into the nature of our experience the more we realize that in truth it is abstract and metaphysical, and that the concrete three-dimensional reality of external 'it' or internal 'I' is only a deceptive mask and an illusion. Take for instance the simple statement 'I am afraid of it'. Supposing I were not afraid of it, the situation would have been changed for me, although 'it' has not changed at all. Reality is not 'it' for me, but what I feel about 'it'. In other words reality for me is in fact my fear of it, which no one has ever seen except as it has been expressed in my panic-stricken action.

Yet panic is not fear, but flight from it. It is as if fear is not really my trouble at all, but only my attitude towards fear, which was too frightened to sustain it, (e.g. fright = fear plus flight). This is pure metaphysics again. It is not it that matters for me, but what I feel about it. And again, not what I feel, but what I feel about what I feel, and what I feel about what I feel about what I feel. Here we are faced with the most unpleasant experience, whether of emotion or philosophy. It is known as an 'Infinite Regress', which is an endless recurring decimal of an abstract metaphysical nature. To those who have thus felt their blood run cold, however, their hearts running away from them, and their stomach dissolved in fire, it is none the less real for that. Perhaps therefore it is not to be wondered at that the plain matter-of-fact man should have taken refuge in the bald, blunt statement, that things are simply what they are, and if we do not see it, it is not there. Metaphysical or otherwise, he feels safer if he says there are no ghosts, in case one might catch him unawares. However, he need not make such a cowardly pretence of attachment to what he hopes is real, because there is another alternative which presents a much simpler and more effective solution.

Let us return to the concept of polarity again. We can realize that we have in polarity a criterion of direction which decides 'which way', whether positive or negative, Yes or No, this way or that way, for or against. Since that fear which we felt for 'it', was itself also a phenomenon of negative polarity (rejection), it is not to be wondered at that the phenomenon of negative polarity should be experienced in regard to fear itself, thereby transmuting fear to flight, and flight to panic, in Infinite Regress. Change of polarity from minus to plus, from No to Yes, from strain to relaxation, from rejection to acceptance, would, however, in spite of its deeply abstract and metaphysical quality, have the immediate and fundamental effect of changing the entire situation, and thus would change the meaning of reality itself. The path is thus to retrace our steps from panic to flight, from flight to fear, from fear to relaxation and acceptance, from regress to progress. The enemy who is thus positively beloved, has changed instantly his very self because our feelings have changed towards him.

It may be only a matter of metaphysics, abstract qualities, unseen causes, dimensional differences, and yet it is the very root and branch of our experience of reality. If we are to be matter of fact and common sense, it is in the deep roots of metaphysics that we have to look for our salvation. Not upwards but downwards, not outwards but inwards, not seen but unseen, not concrete but abstract, shall we find the cause.

Reality of Metaphysics

In reality, it is our attitude towards experience that counts. Positive or negative, open palm or clenched fist, it is a metaphysical and abstract matter that makes the difference. There are also other ways in which the abstract is all-important in our valuation of experience. As we fallaciously concede the importance of 'cause' to external events, we fail to notice that what we are seeing as external, is actually reflected from ourselves, as if within a mirror. For instance, if we say: 'You are hateful,' we mean: 'I hate you because you are unkind to me'; and then there are two very important inward assumptions besides the outward fact, to which belong the prior significance of cause. The first is, 'You ought to be kind to me'. (If I did not believe that, then I should not hate you for being otherwise). The second is that the actual experience of unkindness is in me and not in you. (That I should hate you is at least my fault as well as yours.) Judgment therefore depends not only upon 'it', but also upon what we assume 'it' *ought* to be.

Another abstract condition of experience that plays

its metaphysical part in determining the nature of reality for us is the criterion of Purpose, which acts as a 'frame of reference' to determine relatively whether any particular experience is good or bad. The value which we attribute to any experience is conditioned by the extent and direction in which it varies from something which we choose to want. If we demanded less of Purpose (e.g. less Progress), life could not be so bad as now it seems to be: a pound would be worth more, and a pain worth less, if the standard of comparison was not so hopefully high.

Although it is difficult for us to realize it, the reality which we experience is inward and unseen. It is an aspect of our 'anxiety about anxiety' that makes us tend to be so apprehensive of the material aspect of external cause. There is something comforting and warm about this external tangible 'it'. It is a convenient scapegoat, this fixed external system, and it is much easier to blame 'it' than to accept our own responsiveness to unseen relationships in a moving world.

Perhaps it is the idle talk of freedom and free-will that has led us so far astray. But relationship implies a loss of it, for where two or three are gathered together someone must suffer inroads upon independence, and membership of any society requires obedience to a strict discipline. Our lives are conditional upon these others, seen or unseen. It is nonsense to talk of freedom, but talk we do, as if it were some right to be jealously guarded against all would-be aggressors. No, we are functions of relationship, four-dimensional beings in spite of ourselves. We are spaced in time: that invisible abstract and metaphysical concept is indeed the hidden master of our lives, from timely birth to just as timely end. There are times when our impulses are untimely and ill-timed; when ill temper brings more heat than light into the lives of those others who, since they have interfered with us (or perhaps might do so) must be put out of our harm's way. Timely or untimely change means all that matters of the difference between Peace and War. In fact, we are at the mercy of our metaphysic. The plain matter-of-fact man may be too blunt to understand as yet, but he too will learn in time that Reality is Time, and Time, relationship. Our metaphysic is our fact; indeed we well may ask, have we any other?

Reality is moving for our experience and sets up a state of anxiety or strain. In order to overcome this, we attach ourselves the more securely to this seen and 'real' world, comforting ourselves with the assurance that we are matter of fact, when as a matter of fact we are nothing of the kind. It is part of the reassurance with which we cover our feeling of weakness, that we should thus devote our attention to the placation of external objects. We feel as if the audience matters most; and, being so small amongst so many greater than ourselves, we start upon our journey with the firm intention of being on the side of the big battalions. Alas for such a simple ruse, for nothing is to be gained by siding with the enemy, if we would ever be ourselves. The matter-of-fact man is in for a bad time. No description of reality could be more metaphysical than that.

Fear

Of late years fear has been much maligned, as if it were a bad thing. But surely if it is defined as 'a feeling of inadequacy' it is a fundamental fact in our experience, and not to be ignored or eliminated as an unworthy judgment upon reality. It has been a habit of careless definition to equate fear with flight, but it would be equally justifiable to equate income with expenditure. Fear is a feeling, an act of cognition, a sentient warning, a statement of fact: it does not necessitate action about itself. The question then arises: What shall we do about it? Although it may look as if the sole possible reaction is a negative one (e.g. fight or flight), the fact remains that the positive acceptance of fear is far more effective, and can in fact be attained. It is then called 'Courage', which is not the opposite of fear, but an attitude of positive acceptance towards the sense of fear. Speaking thus accurately with balanced words, it is therefore not true to say that love, which is unconditional acceptance, casts out fear. It casts out flight, by adopting a positive attitude about fear. As an attitude towards fear, it resolves it within a greater love, as the negative is changed into the positive.

It does not seem too much to claim that normal growth occurs 'in the fear of God'. Star-pattern, from seed to bud and bud to flower; from egg to chick and chick to bird; from babe to child and child to man: we possess this positive attitude of expansion in face of the unknown, living in despite of circumstances. In vital circulation, at the mercy of the unseen, we can yet live generously, timely, fitly, 'waiting upon the Lord'. Thereby we might omit much of that aggressiveness which comes either from lack of fear, of common sense or of good manners.

Although much of our most modern teaching has aimed at eliminating fear, this is not entirely due to the New Testament emphasis upon love. The Old Testament constantly emphasized the wisdom of the fear of God. How can we be anything else but afraid, if we are to be true in our judgment of life? If we are wise, however, we shall not let that worry us, but we shall accept and relax, being as positive as we can about it. Defining fear as a feeling of inadequacy, we can then the better see the point of defining love as an attitude of unconditional acceptance, in spite of the feeling of inadequacy.

Thinking

While we are considering the two different polar attitudes in regard to anxiety, we may see more clearly how this process affects our way of thinking. This also seems to have escaped the distinction of analysis into its essential duality, for there is more in thought than can be accurately expressed in the assumed unity of a single word. There are, however, two quite different aspects of thinking, which may be classified as follows:

Thinking Plus	Thinking Minus
Cognitive	Conative
Passive	Active
Watching	Doing
Incoming	Outgoing
Light	Heat

Negative or active thinking is therefore a form of purposive behaviour which urgently insists upon inter-

93

ference with reality. Thus involved in change, it most frequently elects to change itself, becoming restless, anxious, doubtful and worried. It is as if the cooler function of thought has become 'hot-headed': and such indeed are the subjective symptoms which in the end result from using our perceptive apparatus as an engine to take the neglected place of deeper drives of power.

If we use the terms 'discrimination' or 'judgment', then the above two aspects of their meaning are included within each of these words, and it is interesting that both of them have tended to lean increasingly in their assumed meaning towards their active (anxious) aspect. If we are told that we have to go to 'judgment', we anticipate something to our disadvantage; and the term 'discrimination' sounds unpleasant, suggesting that it must be followed by the word 'against', as if someone has been anxious about us, and is trying a policy of punitive extermination. The same applies to 'criticism', which also suggests its negative meaning. But in fact all these words are kinder and more balanced than their usage sounds. The active process of punishment or revenge is a meaning which has been added, and a bias which has been twisted into words that are at least equally significant of a passive process of balanced justice and illumination without moral interference. But we live in anxious days, and many other words ('common' and 'peer', for example) thus show the influence of infinite regress, towards the material, competitive and aggressive side of meaning.

How many of us can really use our thought process as an illuminant, without moral bias or egotistic distortion? The tendency is all in favour of the active interfering kind of thinking, which creates upon the mental screen an illusionary world, preferable in so many of its details to that reality which exists beyond. The process of thinking in terms of wish fulfilment, creative as it is of comforting fallacy, might almost be called 'political thinking', because it seems to be the way in which the minds of those preoccupied with the social needs of others must operate. The other kind of thought is the process of illumination which belongs to the scientific method, rare in all of us and characteristically lacking in any kind of moral discrimination, selective choice, act of so-called free-will or egotistic enterprise. Such goodwill, however, seems to demand an attitude towards life that is beyond the limits of ambitious leaders, because it can never coexist with the more active forms of egotism.

The error of the plain matter-of-fact man, who hoped that he could fix his reality in terms of material facts and unmoving definitions, seems also to have infected the psychologists, who should have known better. Attachment to any system, whether psychological or otherwise, is suggestive of anxious escape from life. Unfortunately, both the plain matter-of-fact man and the psychologist are able to shield themselves under the claim that they are being the more scientific, because they are thus ignoring the unseen. There is a certain smug self-righteousness about this abhorrence of metaphysics. Metaphysic is so near to truth, that it never can be popular with anxious minds. Some people cannot think of the word 'metaphysical' without prefacing it with 'too', and we are not surprised to read in

The Oxford English Dictionary that this is another of the words (like mystical) which are often used with abusive intention. Thus when we get too near to truth for the safety of our cherished phantasies, we bring rudeness to our aid, whether we are politicians, psychologists or men-in-the-street.

Feeling and Emotion

In regard to the next item for analysis, however, even the Dictionary itself fails to help us. It is as if in this, as well as in many other ways, our understanding has to travel beyond the limits of habitual language and conventional meaning. In the case of the process of thought itself, we found no words to make clear the distinction between its cognitive and conative aspects. In general, however, language is kinder to us and there are usually two words in common usage to distinguish between two such different meanings, although very often the ignorant and careless may use them both as synonyms, so that even the Dictionary must loosely follow current usage.

Confusion is always significant if we regard it from the angle of potential purpose. It is the common habit of both layman and expert to use the words 'Instinct' and 'Intuition' as if they meant the same, from which we may infer an instinctive preference for the former, and doubt in regard to the latter. Yet Instinct is as low as Intuition is high: the one is heat, the other light. Instinct is a tendency to action, but Intuition is a sensitiveness to judgment from experience; the former is partial and the latter total; in all respects of our analysis, these two are opposites, and yet they are confused as one. Our ignorance of Intuition is in fact so great, that we may infer it must be purposive, in order to protect us from this feared faculty of experiencing the reality of the unseen. Here is a flight from fact, expressed in words of common usage.

We are at peace through Intuition, but at war by Instinct. The same applies between Feeling and Emotion, for here also the same confusion commonly occurs. Yet Feeling is cognitive (incoming) and Emotion is conative (outgoing), and they are poles apart. Feeling, like intuition, is a state of sensitiveness, but emotion is a tendency (instinctively, aggressively, urgently) to do something about it. Seeing that sensitiveness is usually related to a state of painful suspense, it is easy to understand our bias in favour of uneasy action, so that emotion is instinctively preferred. Although there can be no peace in our emotions, yet we can feel peaceful, in spite of the external threat of War.

Although the distinction between these two words is as important as that which exists between Income and Expenditure (which surely should not be confused) and is essential for an accurate analysis of Peace and War, yet in *The Oxford English Dictionary* Feeling is defined as 'the state of being emotionally affected: emotional attitude'. Emotion, however, is defined as 'a state of stirring, agitation, or passion: psychologically, a feeling, e.g. of desire'. It seems strange that so little account should be paid in common usage to our state of peace in regard to reality, as distinct from the warlike tendency to do something about it, prompted by our own desire for wish fulfilment. There is surely something here which needs some deeper

G 97

DIAGRAM 9

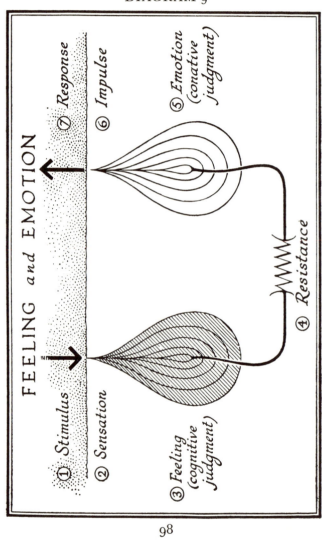

FEELING *and* EMOTION

① Stimulus

② Sensation

③ Feeling (cognitive judgment)

④ Resistance

⑤ Emotion (conative judgment)

⑥ Impulse

⑦ Response

understanding, and clear 'cognitive' thinking. That which we lack, namely, broadmindedness and toleration, such as is exemplified by the scientific method, depends upon this peaceful capacity to evaluate without interference, to be sensitive without doing anything about it. Perhaps we are gradually in process of learning a new attitude towards life, which involves this accurate analysis between feeling and emotion. But it seems we have not learnt it yet, either in our public habits, or in the common usage of our language.

Our learning is an up-hill task, however, because we are instinctively intolerant of that state of suspense in which the sensitiveness of our feelings must always involve us. This instinctive tendency to resolve suspense by means of flight from feeling has resulted in a habit of defensive 'tabu' upon feeling. It is something to be despised, because we feel sure that feeling ought not to exist (but note the contradiction), and that its place should be taken by superior reason. The fallacy goes further, and we judge that, because women feel more and men think more, therefore men must be the superior sex. The morally defensive bargain which we have made with an offensive reality has thereby become conveniently rationalized; that which we chose for safety's sake has now also become morally recognized as best. It is noteworthy how often this automatic process of burglar becoming policeman is successful, as a solution of our possible discomfiture.

Diagram 9 (page 98) is drawn to show the point of tension which exists, where this analysis between feeling and emotion is fairly made. Above the horizontal line is 'Not-self', separate from Self; to the left of the vertical line is Income (cognition), to the right Expenditure (conation), which is the second necessary analysis. On the left-hand side (1) external stimulus (2) arouses sensation, which is then distributed in the psyche in such a way as to create (3) a 'feeling' or 'judgment' about the external situation. On the right-hand side the outgoing path of the nervous impulse is traced from (5) emotion, through (6) impulse, until there is (7) some eventual response either physically, inside the body, or externally, through behaviour in regard to the environment. It is at (4), the bridge or 'synapse', that the condition of strain is felt.

It is important to relate the psychological with the neurological aspect of this problem. It seems as if the nervous system of some people finds it extremely difficult to maintain a state of strain at this nerve junction or synapse, without overflowing from one side of the bridge to the other. These are the ill-balanced people whom we are accustomed to call 'hypersensitive' or 'highly strung'; or if we judge them by their defensive activities, 'emotional' or 'hysterical'. In fact there is no doubt that our judgment is never in favour of these emotional people, but it is always in favour of those who are restrained, balanced, self-contained, and deep instead of superficial. It proves the poverty of later psychological development, however, that of recent years the only alternative to this ill-balanced emotional overflow has been generally considered to be the equal error of emotional repression.

It is true that these two, emotional expression and repression, are opposite to one another. But there is another psychological attitude which is in itself opposite to them both: namely, instead of impulse being allowed to travel unchecked without resistance across the bridge or synapse, something may happen on the left-hand side of the diagram, which enables balance to be maintained without calling upon the emotional response at all. Through an attitude of positive relaxation, the 'onion skin' of sensitive self may grow. Thus the sensitiveness of feeling or awareness may be intensified by a process of inward expansion, for which the proper description seems to be 'suffering' or 'acceptance'. In other words, it is possible to want something very much and yet not to make a fuss if we do not get it, although we still want it. Also it is possible to suffer a great disturbance of feeling, either of pain or pleasure, without bursting into tears or laughter or doing anything whatsoever about it in order to change the strain either of inward or outward state. It is not that we require to preserve the impassivity of poker-face, but merely that good manners and good sense realize that feeling (like many other things) should most frequently be preserved *in situ* and in silence. The outbreak into emotion belongs to a world of sentimentalism and sensationalism, which does not believe in the essential probity of the unseen, but would have all things undressed in the public eye and served up to breakfast with a kipper. But thus to insist that the unseen should be seen is to make it seem obscene, which it need not be if it is allowed to dwell in its proper place.

The emphasis upon emotion must of course inevitably lead to a degree of intolerant interference, which is the early phase of war. If we feel that which is true for us, then it is within our own selves that we suffer, and no one else is involved thereby. But if we become emotional about it, then experience is being external-ized and someone else must share the privilege of our suffering. Sensationalism, sentimentalism, emotional-ism, lack of self-control, a habit of blaming others and of most unphilosophical emphasis upon external cause, all go together to induce a final state of war. We balance our inward instability by insisting upon some external change.

It is instructive that this whole aftermath of con-sequent war has developed out of a situation the original purpose of which was self-defence. Because we could not bear the strain, this war-like process was first set in being; it then must grow as vicious circles do, because the end result is larger strain than that which first initiated it. If we could only learn to bear the beginning of these troubles sensitively within our-selves, there would be less argument and our external troubles would decrease instead of grow upon us as they do. This idolatry of external cause and change, devised instinctively as it was for safety's sake, has propagated that very danger which it was planned to avoid. But being so sick of war, physicians are now try-ing to heal us by a double dose of our disease.

Nerves

Now that we have made this diagnosis of diseased physicians, we are in a better position to understand what is meant by the general term 'Nerves' or 'Nerv-ousness'. This is no mere material error, no fault of the physical system *per se*, no sickness on the part of nervous tissue which has become 'frayed' or 'worn out'. It is an error of attitude, and therefore metaphysical rather than material. It is a process of escape by means of a general negative reaction of rejection, employed unconsciously and instinctively as a mechanism of the psyche and the nervous system, both in body and mind. The basic concept of polarity makes plain the double possibility of the two alternatives. We can react to our experience within ourselves either by Yes or No, and it is the prerogative of 'nerves' to choose the negative reaction, preferring fight or flight instinctively, in self-defence.

Thus nerves will choose and will say 'Yes' to that which is good, but 'No' to everything else, operating a selective trapdoor to experience, by which all is shut out that the nervous individual believes might make him suffer. Nerves are a process of escape from all but the better half of life, and the neurotic is the one who is obsessed by this selective mechanism, which would involve him in flight from so much of experience. Because fear is bad, therefore it must be fled; because anxiety involves suspense or uncertainty, therefore it must be avoided; movement and feeling may perhaps lead to some painful situation, and therefore must not be allowed to happen. All must be fixed and safe in the idolatry of what is seen upon the surface.

Darkness and ignorance are evil, because they may contain the unseen. Therefore actively we must think and know, and all questions ought to have an answer, all problems must be solved. Space is to be avoided because it suggests the possibility of the entry of unseen evil; death must be very bad, because it is a constant threat; the unseen must give way to the seen, and flux to fixity. Amongst the other lesser evils must be added all such adversaries as devils, dragons, demons, serpents, and snakes, and the most mysterious evil of all, woman, who contains within herself all the evils in the list.

In general the attitude exemplified by this negative state of mind is *either* This *or* That. The co-existence of any two such alternatives in a state of suspense conjoined by AND is one which cannot be tolerated. This peculiar state of mind is one which is shared alike by individuals and nations, and leads to much the same behaviour in either case. Being unable to bear the reality which is presented to them, these neurotic escapeologists, masquerading in moral self-justification, decide that something must be done about it; and of course it must be done at someone else's expense. Interference with the course of nature, however, even in so good a cause, unfortunately only projects the intolerable conflict one stage further afield. A negative attitude towards life, always anxious to eliminate the offender, introduces us again to the concept of the Infinite Regress. The war to end war is carried a stage further when aggressiveness aggressively eliminates aggressiveness, and the sword is used to expel the sword for using the sword. The vicious circle can only be broken by the introduction of a different attitude towards life, which will change No to Yes, aggression into acceptance, and nerves into a more tolerant passivity of suffering.

Nerves are NO's. The close parallelism between external and internal events is very simply illustrated by the way in which the sound of a slamming door transmits the negative impulse throughout the whole nervous system of a 'nervy' subject. It feels as if the whole psyche is being slammed in self-defensive detail, as every door and window within the self is instantly closed against potential aggression. The door slams both inside and out, and we describe the sensation as one of 'shock'. The polar relationship persists throughout the whole psyche as well as the central nervous system, and throughout all the parts of it. The reaction of self-defence precipitates a negative response, which shows itself not only in the psyche in one form or another of hysteria, but also throughout the whole physical organism by means of one of the many hysterical reactions of disease.

Disease is defence against dis-ease. Instinctively, negatively and defensively; unconsciously and yet morally and rationally, we are again launched upon a path of infinite regress when we call in the doctor to defend us against our own defensive system. The healer is he who is able to enable us to relax, opening again our positive response which had been closed by some previous shock. The lesson is particularly important for those who are interested in the preventative aspect of disease; namely, that no stimulus should ever be stronger than either mind or body can afford positively to accept. There should be much more emphasis therefore upon rest and quiet, in a civilization the unrest of which is almost entirely expressed in urgent ceaseless action. As we are at present, it is as if an organization, the nature of which is essentially vertebrate, is becoming turned increasingly by its instinctive habit of self-defence towards that other organization of the crustaceans, who would defend themselves against experience by developing an impermeable outward shell. The advantage of the vertebrate over the crustacean is at the expense of increased sensitiveness, but a dispirited neurotic soul likes to feel himself safe behind a wall that does not move.

There are, therefore, many who are neurotic without showing it, or knowing it, and this applies to nations as well as to individuals. Nations as well as men, may be sick in mind as well as body. Those who seek the doctor are those who are discontented with their state; but there is nothing to prevent a neurotic from being pleased with himself for a time, or from passing on his troubles to others under the disguise of moral fervour, or from disturbing other nations on the plea that it is for their welfare.

Many patients who come to the doctor labelled as neurotic, having an insufficiently strong organization to be able to withstand the shocks of life except by means of this defensive method of passing them on to somebody else, have had the negative reaction induced in them by the aggressive habits of those who brought them up. The really ardent neurotics are able to get away with it, because they are so busy doing something about their own disease. They push causes, because they cannot abide at home; they live parasitic lives, either upon their families or upon the society in which they live. Life cannot be cheated, however, and someone must pay the price. Rewards and punishments are not distributed according to our ideas of fairness, but they are nevertheless inexorably reaped by someone in the end, without much reference to who has earned what. In a neurotic society, operating according to the well-worn principle of infinite regress, the successful ones are the more able to satisfy their sense of self-importance by praising themselves for their success, whilst on the other hand they must blame the criminal and diseased for their failure to succeed. All who succeed in society agree that they are 'normal', because they can live successfully under 'normal' circumstances. Those others who fail are labelled 'abnormal', because they are so obviously inferior. Thus morals are satisfied, as they always are, when it has been satisfactorily proved that I am up and You are down, which is through My virtue and Your fault. It should be possible, however, to see a little farther into the process of rewards and punishments, than does this attitude of self-satisfied and self-complacent self-deception.

Tolerant Sensitiveness

It is not possible to over-estimate the importance of emotion in regard to peace and war. Where there is emotion, there will be war, for emotion is the hot-bed and the breeding-ground of warlike gesture and action. To solve the problem of war we must first solve this problem of emotion. But if that is to be done it is not by means of repressing or ignoring or eliminating emotion, but rather by expanding our capacity to feel accurately and sensitively the full meaning of experience. This requires, however, more than most of us at present seem to be capable of; namely, willingness to tolerate that which we dislike, and ability to hold in abeyance the strength of our own desires. To feel sensitively, without becoming emotional, requires this capacity to stand on one side and watch the self objectively. But for most of us there is an identity between Self and Desire, as there is at the same time an identity between Wanting and Having, linked in either case by the word 'ought'. There is always this tendency to unify, and to jump across the bridge or gap, which has the significance of the separative negative. Suspense is so intolerable to us, that the state of the bow with the cord plucked back must instantly be eased by the discharge of the arrow into some target. Thus male must equate with female in a seeming unity which denies the truth of both.

When we feel inclined to jump this gap and to identify ourselves with that external object which we love or fear, we must learn to hold it. It is not enough merely to repress emotion, but we must learn also to expand within ourselves as the wiser alternative. There is so much of this false identification with its resultant mechanism of projection, that we have to learn that even kindness is not enough, because of the false equation which it suggests between self and not-self, you and me. This is the fallacy of Humanism, which has brought it so much disrepute. Interest in the welfare of others, individual or collective, past, present or future, much praised as it has been in the past for moral virtue, is now seen to have been motived very largely, although not always entirely, by this false equation.

Interest in the welfare of our fellow men is not enough, unless we would truly love them as ourselves. Often this telling phrase is twisted into a justification for making a false equation, but its deeper meaning suggests that if we would do so, we can see ourselves in other people. What we must then do is to internalize our observations, referring all such knowledge back to the sources from which it came, within ourselves. It is certainly not enough to do unto others as we would they should do unto us, if by doing so we assume that they are like us and would choose as we ourselves would choose. The only safe assumption is that we are all different, with differences which require to be respected, even when those differences are in apparent disagreement. It is not enough to agree with our friends, we must also agree to differ from our enemies.

Self-Expression

There is so much power within us all, compressed as the spirit within this material manifestation of body-mind, that we very easily claim the right, in fact the moral command, to do something about it. There is so much of value, so much of impelling importance, so much essential 'I' in material 'Me', that our conceit is very liable to transfer values from the inner to the outer world. It is partly self-conceit and partly the self-defence of anxiety in flight from suspense, which adopts this attitude of evoking with moral encouragement that which would be better if left latent and unseen.

It is true that there is this magic power within the self, although we often seem to doubt it. In our anxiety to justify ourselves, we lay premature claim upon the office of this inward Geni, calling him up to be of service, to go and do something for us. It is not that Aladdin is not possessed of a lamp, it is not that we have no magic carpet, because we certainly have. We are extremely unwise, however, when we call upon them, because they are best left to call upon us. (Diagram 10, page 111.) The Geni should be kept in the bottle and the smoke of emotion should be kept constrained within the fire of feeling. It is all a matter of our discipline in time. This power is not to be repressed as evil Dæmon, nor to be evoked as beneficent Geni, but to be expressed as Genius within the limits of the Law. The art of living is not that we may be absolved from action, but rather that action may itself take place accurately in space and time, without that urgent interference which would displace it as a result of our anxious egotism and uneasy flight from fact.

We are bigger than we think, and it only requires a little experience of the reality of paradox to realize that the alternative to active interference is not necessarily complete inertia. Analysis must go with us to the end, so that we can realize that there are two ways even in the act of death. We think of death negatively, either as nothingness or the unseen, but there is another more positive point of view in regard to this experience. In the course of phasic change from one aspect of rhythm to another, we swing from day to night and back again, and from rest to action. We may therefore regard death as being a process in continuity with our present experience, representing only a different phase, negative it now seems to us, but one to be treated positively, accepted and fully welcomed when the time comes. This positive attitude towards death is a very different matter from that aggressive negation of experience which is more dead than death, because it denies the

DIAGRAM 10

THE GENI IN THE BOTTLE

EMOTION

"I must let go!"

FEELING

"I can hold it"

positive value even of death itself, as well as life, which it pretends to hold more dear. There is something worse than death, which is that death when due should be denied. That which is taken positively in due time, however evil it may seem, can never be evil in experience, because nothing is evil except that our negative attitude makes it so. There are many in life more dead than those who learn to adopt this way of life, which dies in due time, thus to create new life in the unseen.

Religion

Seeing that the Geni is the spirit of the matter, now to be returned to store for safer keeping and to safeguard misuse, how does this affect our belief in and practise of Religion? There can be no doubt that religion in practice does provide the best, indeed the only final, guarantee against anxiety. But religion (by our attitude to it, again) may be false or true: and if the former, doubly dangerous because it removes our only source of strength in times of stress and crisis.

For our purpose at this point, it is the method, or attitude to life, that religion implies that is important. We may therefore define religion as 'Acceptance of the Unseen', which emphasizes the attitude of unconditional love.

In practice, religion is the experience of the unseen, but it subdivides again, according to its visible (exoteric) and invisible (esoteric) aspects. The exoteric aspect corresponds with the right bank of the river. There we should expect to find idolatry, priestcraft, theology, Churchianity and all the fearful sticklers and fixers of belief. It is not that Priests and Churches are wrong: it is that we are not to be trusted with them, unbalanced as we are. No knowledge of the truth will prevent us from misusing it. It is not truth we need, but balance, which we are more likely to achieve if we have more faith than belief, and do not feel too sure of any of our facts.

Religion should be a pawn but not a peg, a plaything but not a privilege, for movement is its very life. It has been the fate of all religions to be crucified, not by their enemies, but by their friends. Human earnestness, so fearfully direct, so anxious to improve, builds monuments to house the living God, and kills him dead within an ornamental prison. Life knows better the true path of worship, and builds a dying altar for a living fire. The spirit is incarnate in a dying frame.

The only safety in the teaching of religion, therefore, is to prefix every statement 'This is not true'. There can be no living truth that we can fix in words, dogmas, beliefs or creeds. These are but cowards' castles, neurotic fallacies that lead to suicide and self-destruction. Words are suggestive, provocative and feeble means to be more humbly used in the service of the flame of truth. They are like lanterns; but they are not the light. They serve 'despite' themselves, where egotists would hope, 'because'.

Fallacies disprove themselves in time. Falsehoods fail, dogmas appear ridiculous, pontifs cease to be regarded as bridges unto God, and Churches crumble in decay. They require no holding-up, or fixing by means of the flying buttresses of a rational defence. That which has lived in course of time must die, to be renewed through that experience.

ANXIETY

But what of our anxiety? This truth is too stern to be encouraging, and that is what we need. Where can we find new spirit for our inspiration, new life to breathe? The answer seems to be, by first meeting death on friendly terms. That is our initiation, our proving of the truth today. Let these things die: the time has come for us to learn from Death the deepest lesson of the way of Life.

CHAPTER III: AGGRESSIVENESS

SUMMARY

Dreams.

Action. Unrest 'causes' interference; analysis of action; graceful and disgraceful; the criterion of Time; action X 3 and X 4.

Aggressiveness. Definition; the Time factor; identification and false assumption; summary.

Reality of Strain. Heraclitus; the bow, the arrow and the target; worry and wish-fulfilment; aggressiveness is a two-edged sword.

Eliminative Fixatives. Burglar and policeman; a list of aggressives; examples of infinite regress in 'normal' society; aggressiveness in religions; the growing points of truth today.

Repression. Inward aggressiveness; or, and; the mannerisms of aggressiveness.

Sex. False unification; narrow-mindedness; the effect of repression is to lose control; the swinging pendulum; psycho-analysis and phallic worship; the morality of libertinism.

Murder. Analysis of motive in infinite regress; morality of the sinner.

Acquisitive Society. The sickness of fixation; God is gold; the equal fallacy of opposites.

AGGRESSIVENESS

Adventure of Life. The effect of flight from movement; war-makers cannot tolerate adventure, therefore the only adventure of life is war.

DREAMS[1]

V. *'Privilege'*

I was on a road leading to the shore of a seaside town, expecting a bombardment at any moment from the enemy fleet. The position was most exposed. Behind me there was a building which looked very strong and safe, but I found out that it was only for privileged people, so I just hid behind it, hoping that I should not be hurt.

VI. *'The Tempest'*

We seemed to be somewhere on the coast of the Mediterranean, but it was as if a peninsula, or even a continent, was between two seas which it divided. We were bathing and I understood that the water was calm on the side on which we were, but very rough on the other side. I was drifting about idly on my back.

Looking down on the calm waters, I suddenly realized that there was a frightful storm blowing up from the other side and that it was overwhelming the bridge of land which separated the two seas. I felt that something catastrophic was about to take place as the land between began to fall to pieces, and I ran away naked as far as I could. I got to some unknown house, but was told that it was full of some terrible disease and I could not stay there.

[1] For comment, see Appendix (page 306).

DREAMS

I said: 'If I were a millionaire, what I would do would be to bring the North Atlantic sea alongside the Mediterranean with a piece of plate glass in between. Then I would be able to swim in the Mediterranean and pretend all the time that I was really swimming in the North Atlantic.'

Chapter III

AGGRESSIVENESS

Action

In our aggressive and impatient world, we think too much, yet do not seem to have time enough to think. There is in us too much heat, too little light; too much activity and too little illumination; too much desire to do, too little contact of surrender with reality. Meanwhile we use our words without due attention to their meaning, and there are many which pass in common usage without clear understanding. The bias of our lives is towards action, as the cure for everything. Yet 'action' may be wise or otherwise, acceptance or escape; it may be 'for' or 'against', identification 'with', or simply 'being'. In fact, action may mean anything of good or ill, and of itself can prove no cure for active ills. 'What shall we do?', insistent question that it is, needs something more before our answer can be effective.

The world in which we live would be so much better if it lost the restlessness and intolerance, which finds in action the solution of its deep unrest. And yet if action itself is also bad, does not the alternative of doing nothing offer an excuse for all kinds of inertia, for every policy of selfish isolation and satisfaction while others are left to strive? Granted that action is unrest, what are we to do about the problems with which we are faced, which without action seem as if they never can be changed? For example, what are we to do about the Slums, or any other blot upon our social landscape? Is there nothing to be said for those pioneers who have gone out in a spirit of adventure and left their mark upon our history?

It is no use merely condemning action and saying that it is only an outward solution of an inward unrest. Action requires analysis into those different kinds, which despite their difference are obscured under the cover of one word. Under the classification of three-dimensional and four-dimensional meanings, the pivot point of this distinction is found in regard to the word 'Time'. We can be brief in coming to this point, and say that action may be either graceful when it is 'in time', but disgraceful when it is beside itself, untimely. The Time factor is that which distinguishes these two forms of action, and yet Time, being in its very nature unseen, is not noticed by those who prefer to adopt the more matter-of-fact attitude towards experience. Perhaps it is regarded as 'too metaphysical' for notice by plain people. If facts are only to be regarded as what is visible and tangible, then there can be no distinction between these two kinds of action. But on the other hand, if Time is the kind of fact that matters most, then there is all the difference in the world between them, and this analysis can be defined.

By another classification there is Relative Action, which is tolerant of that to which the action refers, tolerant of time and space and difference, accepting all these facts as part of the reality of the situation; and there is also Absolute Action, which is independent, grandiose, impatient and intolerant of everything but its own inward urge for immediate self-expression. Action which is 'an act of grace' arises as a process of growth out of the related factors in the situation; being well timed, it is kindly and impregnated with its own beauty and originality. Action which is out of place, however, is armed with its own aggressive self-assertive sword, impatiently inflicting itself upon its circumstances. Almost certainly it will be dressed in moral garments for approval, because there is so much need for action that there is no difficulty whatever in claiming that here is something which certainly 'ought' to be done, not only for the benefit of any particular one, but also for the sake of the community. It is for this reason that the analysis of action so readily escapes the deeper criticism of reality. It is in fact 'good' actions which cause most of the harm amongst which we must find our tangled way, because it is in regard to the 'good' (i.e. desirable), that we are most impatient and therefore most likely to escape from the limitations of time and fitness. Therefore it is that so much of good intention becomes 'disgraceful' in the light of history.

Another analysis of this same problem of action makes distinction on the one hand between that action which is spontaneous, a positive flowering or growth (being), and on the other that which is action about action, involving what has been described in the last chapter as an 'infinite regress'. Action can be still more active (and therefore more morally commendable) when it is action about action, or action about action about action, until we become involved in a hyperactive system of activity about activity about activity about activity, *ad infinitum*, down the endless avenues of infinite regress.

This kind of activity is very active and may be extremely virtuous in intention, but being in its nature negative it is in consequence ultimately destructive, for no good thing can ever grow out of a negative attitude towards life. Our analysis of action therefore resolves itself into the following summary:

Action A	*Action B*
X 4	X 3
Timed	Impatient: timeless
Growing	Artificial
Relative	Absolute
Graceful	Disgraceful
Spontaneous	Repressive
Relaxation	Tension
Sensitiveness	Insensitiveness
Positive	Negative (infinite regress)
Compassion	Depression
Love	Hate
Growth	Aggressiveness
Action	Action
Change	Change

Although these two columns indicate a fundamental difference between the two types of action, it must not be forgotten that both may appear to be equally virtuous from the viewpoint of morality. Granted that it is a good thing to move from here to there, about which all may be agreed, the question which remains fundamentally important is: 'Yes, but in what time?' The process may be compared to that of seed and

bomb, the difference being one of speed and relationship. In education for instance, are we to become
grown up or to be blown up? By this measure of our
time is determined the measure of our aggressiveness.

Aggressiveness

'Aggressiveness is energy applied to reduce time and /
or space between subject and desired objective.' This
definition includes growth, which is movement step by
step in natural time, and introduces the simplest deri-
vation of the word 'aggressiveness' (Lat. *ad*, towards;
gradior, I step). This cannot be all, however, that is
meant by aggressiveness, for it is not from such graceful growth that we have ever suffered. As desire is more
hasty, beating time anxiously, so aggressiveness increases in its pathology until, when time is altogether
eliminated, it has reached its maximum.

It is important to notice that through a continuous
process of time elimination, the significant value of
aggressiveness has changed from positive on the one
hand to negative on its opposite extreme, and from
contructiveness in growth to destructiveness when time
has been eliminated. The seed is the symbol of all
that grows in time, but the bomb is the symbol of all
that timelessness destroys.

Normal growth occurs in space-time by means of a
relationship between the positive and the negative, or
between desire and resistance. Thus the negative resistance is first 'accepted', and then in time grown
through. By this process of growth we are always involved within a discipline, facing an unknown, and
active in a state of suspense [see Diagram 11 (a)]. There

DIAGRAM 11

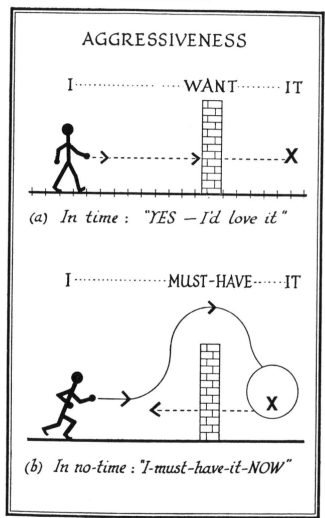

AGGRESSIVENESS

I ········· ···· WANT ········ IT

(a) *In time* : *"YES — I'd love it"*

I ············· ···MUST-HAVE·····IT

(b) *In no-time* : *"I-must-have-it-NOW"*

124

AGGRESSIVENESS

is something that we want which is beyond us: life is like an open question, the unknown answer to which involves anxiety, which for our normality in this experience requires most positive acceptance. Contrasted with this is the abnormal state of anxious urgency: 'I must-have-it-NOW,' which is the condition illustrated in Diagram 11 (b). In this the strain of anxious suspense is felt to be intolerable and both space and time are jumped by means of a false assumption, which can the more readily be believed within the facile screen of consciousness, because it can be so easily moralized by conscience into a sense of duty. 'I want it; I must have it now; I ought to have it now because it is good; it ought to be mine now; in fact it is mine now, and who denies that is my hateful enemy.' Upon the screen of consciousness we can draw so many pictures of our own reality, which are the more intensely held as belief, because they represent desire achieved. No wonder, then, that we are anxious not to have opinions changed or prejudices cured. We hold to what we have, from fear of that unseen which would rob us of our fond illusion. 'Do not tell me the truth, for I am precariously balanced by my own beliefs.'

Diagram 12 on the next page illustrates (c) the possibility of relationship between two moving systems, connected as it were by cogs, fitting one into the other each in time. The normal process of growth is that the motive power from each of these two systems should operate within itself in spite of this relationship. Watch, however, what happens if the larger system on the left-hand side of the page becomes over-active in its sense of duty, and starts to rotate the smaller system to

DIAGRAM 12

RESISTANCE

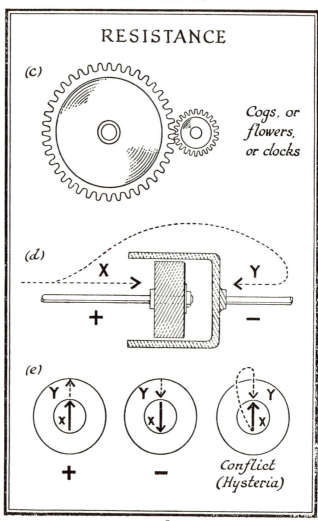

(c)

Cogs, or flowers, or clocks

(d)

X > Y <

+ —

(e)

Y ↑ Y ↓ Y ↓ x ↑

+ — *Conflict (Hysteria)*

which it is related. The motive power is then external and not internal, and the actor has in this sense become a puppet of the audience, or the child a movement of its parents' motor.

This problem may be further illustrated from diagram (d) in which a moving system (X) is met by a resistance, or more slowly moving system (Y). Growth will then be a process of expansion of X within Y, in which Y is moved outwards in time. This process may be continuous, as X gradually overcomes the resistance of Y, so that its movement may gradually extend to cover the whole of Y's system; or on the other hand, the relationship of these two systems may be an alternating rhythm, such as occurs in the piston and cylinder, in which X rises and falls as the resistance of Y diminishes or relatively increases. As a third alternative, the force of X may be less than that of the resistance which it meets from Y, so that Y may gradually overwhelm its lesser neighbour. These three alternatives may again be referred to Diagram (e) in which on the left-hand side there is a movement from X to Y, as Y's resistance is gradually resolved (positive phase), whereas the next diagram shows what happens when the resistance of Y is too great and the system is therefore moving in a negative phase. In the third diagram the two forces are in conflict, and altogether out of time relationship or harmony. (This problem is worth special consideration in regard to the movements of partners in ballroom dancing.)

To return to the earlier illustration, Diagram 11 gives a more personal flavour to the problem, where the 'Little man' walking along the time-track of experience is faced by the resistance of some obstruction in his path, between him and the desired objective. On the one hand (a) his attitude is graceful, tolerant and disciplined, so that feeling 'Yes, I'd love it,' he still retains his place in space and time, moving gracefully towards his desired objective if he can. Compared with him his more urgent neighbour (b) in the lower part of the diagram, finds morality more activating than reality, and phantasy than fact. He feels so sure that he ought to have it and therefore assumes that it is his now, jumps the wall, possesses himself of it and finds that he has thus gained a dubious advantage. He must now adopt a negative attitude, because he has thus identified himself with that which was so negative to him. The arrows of direction have become reversed, through an intolerance of this fundamental fact of time. This will always be found to be the case, for although growth (in time) is positive, timeless aggressiveness is negative. There is so much instruction to be gained from this fact, that it is surprising that the significance of time should be omitted from our philosophy. Yet if we look at the methods of our education, whether in nurseries, schools, religion or politics, there is still too little known of the deep discipline of time.

There is so much moral virtue to be easily acquired by beating the clock, that it is difficult to realize that such ardent endeavour is evidence only of the un-weaned state of egotistic insistence upon the right to have timelessly, hastily, securely, NOW. Such aggressiveness will be the very enemy of truth and peace, yet it is only time that separates it from the natural process of growth in grace. It is dangerously easy to transfer the values that belong to system A (i.e. four-dimensional reality, eternity, spirit or the whole) from A to system B (three-dimensional reality, space, time, the material part), where they do not belong. 'Me' assumes the quality and value of 'I', and Me's egotism thus enjoys a universal importance, which is the prerogative not of Me but of I. (This is vanity, idolatry, neurosis or untruth.)

'I want it now!' These desired objectives seem to assume so much external value in their own right, but we must learn to regard them as meaningless and valueless in themselves, being only mirrors projecting some deeper value upon our vision. That deeper value is not external but internal, and is derived not from external B but from internal A. 'It' is the means to the end that I should be that which I am: which is not Me. Yet anxiety will always persuade us otherwise, offering us trick solutions, showing us vain causes, asserting moral compulsion to achieve some impossible promise in the name of some mythical respectability. Here is our problem, and it is a matter of Time.

It is this same matter of an attitude towards Time that makes all the difference between the behaviour of two passengers in the same bus. They may both be late for an appointment, yet one is jumping up and down in his seat, as if by so doing he thinks that his activity will be transmitted to the driver and the engine. His state of mind, aggressively pushing within the slowly moving bus, makes no more difference to the time at which it arrives at its destination, however, than does the mood of his more relaxed and easy-going companion, who is able to enjoy the passing scene in spite

I   129

of the fact that he cannot make it move any faster. If this restless one is only a passenger, he is less likely to do harm than if, as is unfortunately too often the case, he is the driver of the vehicle. In that case, being more independent, he is more free to 'step on it', causing his presumptuous over-activity to collide disastrously with less impatient travellers upon the way of life. 'Beating the clock' is not really to be regarded as a virtue because, under whatever guise it travels, its destructiveness will account for the slaughter of mankind, which is left as tragic litter upon the path of this impatient self-assertive Juggernaut.

To summarize before leaving this very important question of the nature of aggressiveness, we may divide it into two kinds:

1. Normal, e.g. timely growth; the seed lives gracefully.

2. Abnormal, e.g. timeless bursting of the bonds of discipline; the bomb.

The latter may again be subdivided into

(a) Timeless defensive identification with the feared object.

(b) Timeless offensive identification with the desired objective.

We may also note that as between these two kinds of aggressiveness:

1. The Time factor is decisive in diagnosis.

2. The two kinds are opposite in sign and value.

3. 'Fitness' in Time is the essential virtue, both for growth and grace.

The Reality of Strain

There is a phrase of Heraclitus: 'The world order is a harmony of opposing tensions, as in the lyre and the bow.' These words so adequately describe the situation in which we find ourselves, that it almost seems unnecessary to go further, either in the definition or in the solution of the problem of living.

If life is truly thus, why not calmly relax and let it be? There is something within ourselves, however, that makes it extremely difficult to realize this frank simplicity; so that, by straining against our state of strain, we are faced with a problem of apparently infinite complexity. By performing an act of infinite regress (action about action about . . .) upon such a simple matter, we have thus multiplied not the creative but the destructive side of life. Where life supplies the intimate conjunction 'and', we have preferred to our moral advantage the more unfriendly 'or'. Since opposites there must be, the way in which we have preferred to solve the problem of this opposition is by opposing it.

Great as is the latent power presented to mankind, we have preferred to use it contrary to the law of life. Why? If we could merely say 'out of stupidity', it would be so much easier; but that is not the case, because it is not stupidity which has made egregious choice. On the other hand, it is knowledge, cleverness, experience, morals, earnestness, benevolence, and such a list of human virtues that it becomes difficult to see how they could have led us so far astray. Well-meaning as our interference seems to be, yet 'sweet' is not the adjective to precede such 'reasonableness'; because as reason is of this pre-selective kind, it must always aggressively choose this or that in its process of comparisons and classifications. Unfortunately for mankind, our desires are still identified with this process of reason. We do not yet realize that it is as much less than life as part is less than whole, and as a three-dimensional system is less than that four-dimensional system, which differs from it by the more tolerant inclusion of its opposites. Reason is like a sword, aggressive, grasping what should be left alone, and separating that which might otherwise come together.

Five thousand years ago, both more and less, the system of polarity was recognized as the basis of life, by those wise men who created from it the tolerant philosophy of wholeness in balance (Tao). But since then progress and civilization have devised a better plan. We have chosen instead to eliminate that opposite, our adversary, calling him Satan the Evil One, thereby reducing everything to a seeming single unity. Since there was this duality, the two parts of which were related across a chasm of separative space, facing one another as enemies, how admirable it must have seemed to equate the difference; not in time but now, not two but one. The only question was: Which one? It cannot be wrong to assume that every such equation depends upon the fact that if I choose, the chosen one cannot be You, but must be Me.

Before our Christian era there was a deeper recognition in high places of the fourth-dimensional reality than has occurred until quite recent years, when science, philosophy and mathematics (but not yet religion) are bringing us back again to the deeper sense

132

of things, with added knowledge which was denied to the intuitive insight of those our wholesome ancestors.

So much of modern civilization and its so-called progress is the same stuff that neurosis is made of. In its ardent escape from fact, it is swiftly impelling society over the brink of bankruptcy and into the chaos of unending war. The world in which we live at the present time is very largely a neurotic one. In fact, at times we may be tempted to use the even ruder label of psychotic, to describe its state of unstable insistence upon the unreal.

But now we feel justifiably worried about the movement of events, and we have the instability of our condition on our minds. That is not enough, however, for all neurotics are bursting with worry and anxiety, and they are also preoccupied with the problems which are on their minds. The question is not whether 'it' is on our minds or not, but *how* it is on our minds. Is our attitude towards it positive or negative; and is this situation of torment and anguish one that we are positively accepting, or are we negatively insisting that it should be changed? It is easy to see why there should be so much crying for peace at a time when the threat of war is imminent, and yet to cry for peace is not in itself enough. It has always been the fallacy of human foolishness to believe that it is possible to eliminate reality by a process of wish-fufilment. 'Take it away, I don't like it', is an eliminative process, a form of aggressiveness, yet being the very seed of war itself, it never can be the cure of it. We may desire peace for either of two reasons: either because we are prepared to live in the way of peace, or because we wish to

133

escape from the conflict which we have brought upon ourselves. From the latter motive, peace would urgently eliminate its enemy war, and thus create not peace but further war. Aggressiveness has never yet been cured by aggressiveness, nor war by war; nor can either be eliminated by any other method than that of love. Only unconditional acceptance of the beloved enemy will absorb him in time into the larger circle of our friends.

Yet humanity leaps instinctively to the solution of claiming peace at the point of the sword. It is a subtle commentary upon the nature of reality that things which are so different as the sword and the cross seem to bear so much superficial resemblance to one another, that we can just as well hit our brother on the head with the cross, as we can insist upon his peacefulness at the point of the sword. We can always claim reasonably and righteously that this is the war to end war, and that with this sword all I intend to do is to disarm you—unless, of course, there should be some misunderstanding about your equally polite intention to do the same for me. It is so reasonable to eliminate the undesirable and get rid of all that may cause our distress. But this sword is similar to the weapon of our consciousness, that also has two sharpened edges. Alas for my benevolence, this sword with which I so reasonably kill you has another edge and another point, upon which I also must inevitably be impaled in time.

Diagram 13 (page 135) is a simpler version of the 'River' diagram on page 65, and shows the change of direction which ensues upon the process of double acceptance, instead of the interference of selective choice.

DIAGRAM 13

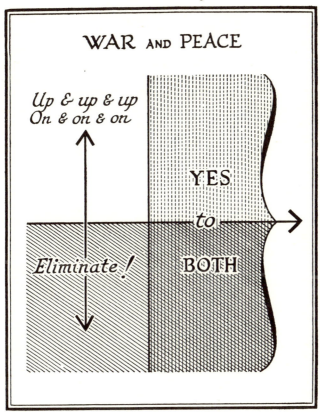

WAR AND PEACE

Up & up & up
On & on & on

YES

to

Eliminate!

BOTH

This is a dimensional difference; and mathematicians of relativity may perhaps wonder whether they can see in it an example of the change which occurs by multiplication of a factor by $\sqrt{-1}$.

AGGRESSIVENESS

Eliminative Fixatives

Who are our most active aggressors in conventional society, and how do they work? It is a truism to say that things are not what they seem. Those who are prepared to look clearly in the face of life must become accustomed to the familiar difficulty of the similarity of opposites, and the fundamental opposition of those things which seem to be similar. Diagram 14 (page 137) illustrates this familiar fact in a simple way. The common denominator which is shared by the two apparently opposing systems of Burglar and Policeman is an insistence upon security and timelessness, at once to be attained and retained. Thus the more highly developed burglar, whose sense of efficiency has grown with experience, realizes that moral burglary has more advantages in its favour than that of any more directly anti-social enterprise. He therefore turns policeman, and collects the swag amidst the encouraging applause of conventional society.

Aggressive but untimely collectors of good things look rather interesting in a heap together. Sharing this in common, but otherwise unfamiliar, their other differences must serve to sort them out:

Burglars	The self-righteous
Policemen	The lazy
Criminals	The too-clever
The punitive law	The conventional
Profiteers	The satisfied
Possessives	The spoilt
Usurers	The discontented
Beggars	The cowards
Suggestibles	The starved
Rebels	The sleepy

DIAGRAM 14

UNITY IN OPPOSITION

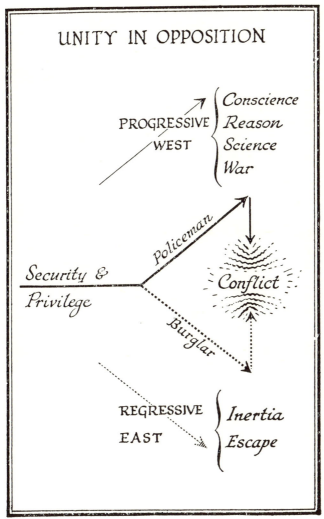

PROGRESSIVE
WEST

Conscience
Reason
Science
War

Policeman

Security &
Privilege

Conflict

Burglar

REGRESSIVE
EAST

Inertia
Escape

AGGRESSIVENESS

Neurotics	Impatient adolescents
The over-conscientious	Aged cynics
Sensationalists	Sentimentalists

Any or all of these are possessed of some degree of infinite regress, which has raised the power of B (the right bank of the river) to the nth dimension. The reader can work out for himself the nature and effect of an attitude of infinite regress in regard to different matters: e.g. burgling, aggressiveness, pain, fear, self-righteousness, knowledge, etc. Some of them may get rather complicated during their rotation about a vicious circle, but if he will imagine in his own mind how such a society would seem if highly organized upon such aggressive lines, then perhaps the picture will form itself into that which he can see in our present 'normal' world.

Disappointing as it may seem to all our phantasies of moral correctness, it is important to realize that the cause of our troubles is not to be found in the mental simplicity of the motive and methods of that wicked Burglar Bill. It is a strong probability that the 'cause' of his trouble was in the unseen to us, long before he ever stepped upon our stage of the seen. But it is part of our plan for happy ignorance, that we should effectively punish Burglar Bill for being the cause of our troubles, by beating him into betterness or clapping him into gaol. The complexity of our intelligence seems to be more than equalled by the depth of our stupidity, and by the extreme blindness of our inability to tolerate reality. There is an aspect of society which is aggressiveness in infinite regress, and even pacifism itself may be one symptom of that negative and distortive process.

ELIMINATIVE FIXATIVES

Religions of the world, at least in their exoteric manifestations and present decadence, offer as good examples of organized aggressiveness as can be found. One of the difficulties over which Christianity has failed has been due to its insistence upon its missionary privilege, based upon such words as: 'As the Father has sent me, so send I you,' (John xx, 21.) Such verbal authority for teaching does not authorize bad teaching, and cannot justify the carrying of the word of the Christian gospel, if not at the point of the sword, at least with the utmost aggressiveness to which reason and morality can consent. There is nothing to be said against the missionary spirit in itself, nor indeed is it justifiable to say anything against any spirit, other than to illuminate the way in which it is employed. The point is that the spirit of this or any other Gospel may be conveyed gracefully as an act of inward illumination, or aggressively as an act of intolerant insistence from outside. Diagram 12, page 126 of the two cogs, is a good illustration of this point.

There can be no justification, either in the Bible or anywhere else, for the missionary spirit being carried in a 'disgraceful' way. Unfortunately, however, being the kind of people that we appear to be, this item of analysis between the good and bad missionary seems to be somewhat obscured. Mohammedism, with the excellent intention of spreading peace, has always carried it in practice at the point of the sword, with the implied ideal of 'the sooner the better', so that it must be rammed down somebody's throat in the most material fashion. Roman Catholicism has often stood for the aggressiveness of an authoritarian restriction, and has been inclined to maintain in her children a state of sub-adolescent dependence upon Mother Church. Puritanism, alive to the errors of the seen, adopted an attitude of moral repression in order to eliminate evil, and has thus become a hot-bed in history for neurotic fixation. The ever-recurrent schismatic process of negative rejection led to compensatory protestations of Protestant reasonableness; and the highly intellectual sermons of the present day do much to obscure the reality of the spirit, behind the screen of a more or less water-tight three-dimensional argument.

Religion everywhere seems to be in the same process of decline. Aggressiveness is balanced by regressiveness, and the same decay which is seen in the West in different forms of aggressiveness is balanced in the East by regressive tendencies towards inertia, where interest in the unseen has led to the adoption of a negative policy of eternal sleep. There is nothing wrong with religions, except the way in which they are manifested in theology and carried out in practice by mankind. The error is with man and it is due to his dislike of the spacial and temporal limits of the nature of his incarnation. His spirit seems to have exceeded the discipline of Time, and his untimely efforts have become moralized beneath a façade of contented self-righteousness.

The purest teaching of the non-aggressive technique, which is timely and illuminative, seems at present to be practised chiefly in three directions, which may therefore be described as the modern growing points of Christianity. These are: (1) the scientific method, (2) certain developments in psychology which best conform thereto (the whole of Jung, but not all Freud), and (3) Zen Buddhism, which is an excellent example of four-dimensional realism.

Repression

We have dealt with many of the external aggressors, but it is now necessary to turn our attention to that inward aggressor, who is the inward image of his external manifestation. Repression is aggressiveness aggressively treated by its elimination. Reality repeats itself, and the same problem exists within the psyche as outside it. Our inward order of 'opposing tensions' is also unfortunately lacking in harmony. Seeing that we are within ourselves not one but two, the same question arises, Which One? There is the same tendency to eliminate one member of this opposing group. As to which is to be the chosen one between ourselves, there is little difficulty in providing the answer. The one we want to be is that which represents the seen aspect of the self, operating in terms of the physical body and its conscious and conscientious (male aggressive) function. We therefore impose a tabu on all that is within the unseen, which includes the inward spirit, the serpent-force, as the source of movement. Thus space, darkness and death; feeling and the female aspect of the psyche; magic and witchcraft, are all included within the same tabu. All these are to be numbered amongst the bad things, because of their vitally disturbing nature to the world of the seen, of which they hold both the key and the roots. In this battle to eliminate the unseen enemy, victory is assumed by morality and reason, by thinking and fixing, by having and doing, and by all that the materially possessive male can hope for in his urgent demand for safety, possessiveness and privilege.

In the name of peace of mind, by means of repression, intolerant of suspense, we provide a false façade of unity, approval and self-righteousness. Behind this, however, there is always lurking the unseen enemy, which contains the seeds of life itself. Thus the negative forces in the psyche hope to have gained a victory over the positive, and the aggressor rules blandly above the submerged head of his own aggressiveness.

The answer to such a process is best described in terms of infinite regress, and leads to that state of psychic unrest in which so many of us find ourselves at the present day. The situation is illustrated in Diagram 13 (page 135) and in Diagram 3 (page 65: 'The River'). On the left-hand side of Diagram 13, the two aspects of the psyche are divided horizontally in terms of opposition between the seen and the unseen. The same bilateral condition is seen on the right-hand side of the diagram with, however, the difference that where on the left the two are held to be in conflict, on the right they are allowed to be in harmony. On the left it was a case of Either *or*, on the right it is This *and* That. On the left, one must be maintained in superiority over the other (repression); but on the right, both are regarded as the very elements of life itself, to be related in abundant harmony. These two attitudes towards life are negative and positive, but it is towards the former that we are most reasonably prone.

If we make a list of the variety of our aggressive mannerisms, which determine the details of this negative attitude, it is impressive in its length:

Fixation	Men
Repression	Mechanization
Conscience	Missionaries
Morals	Idealists and Progressives
Honour	Faddists
Loyalty	Amusement, (B-musement?)
Action	Invalidism
Organization	Pacifism
Efficiency	Humour
Freedom	Teasing
Rights	Reason

Of course it is not intended in any way to belittle such activities of the spirit as are prepared to flower within the discipline of accepted limitations, and thus to grow. The above list may be added to indefinitely, because in all things it is possible to adopt the aggressive attitude, but in themselves there need not be anything wrong with any item. For example, a sense of humour is inserted because so much of humour is unkind, being engaged largely in laughing aggressively at something, instead of smiling tolerantly with it (i.e. the laugh is external and negative, instead of internal and positive). Jokes of a sexual kind supply the material for so much of what is loosely called a sense of humour, but they are in fact the strongest indication of the lack of it in the deepest sense. Wherever humour is forced in any way, it may be suspected that it is behaving as a function of aggressiveness, rather than according to the laws of kindlier growth.

If the reader should feel that any one of the items

listed above has been unfairly placed, the covering grace of inverted commas will show more clearly that it is only the aggressive aspect of this virtue which is being selected for our disapproval. (There is of course no doubt that we may disapprove. The point is that we may not force change upon the objects of our disapproval. We may change them, but not by force: all true change is an emanation of growth through fertilization by love.)

Sex

The higher art of sex is most intimately a matter of truth in time, because it requires a genius for relationship. Since sex is the prototype of all polar relationships, it is obvious that aggressiveness must have peculiar bearing upon our attitude towards this aspect of our experience. Again, aggressiveness may operate in two opposing ways, either positively or negatively, and —as is usually the case—the one with which we are more familiar is the negative aspect. All narrowmindedness is aggressive. The narrowness of 'Puritanism' and 'Calvinism', which exploit morality, conscience and guilt, thereby adopt an aggressive attitude towards sex, in order that it should be utterly eliminated.

Narrowmindedness, in self-defence, always maintains that there should be no allowance for the operation of this evil impulse, apart from its expression through certain morally desirable and socially valuable channels. Sex is therefore something to be both elevated into phantasy and subjugated out of fact, perverted and sublimated, to suit our sense of privilege and at the same time eliminate all sense of difference and danger. The effect of such an attitude towards sex must of course be to release the repressed obverse, to operate unseen in some way which is dissociated from the recognized normal channels of human behaviour. That is always the way with those who thus impetuously decide to ignore the unseen. By saying that it is not there, they set it free to run amok and bite them in the back.

Our progress since those dark and unenlightened days of our Victorian parentage (but were they really so dark as ours today?) has been as rapid as the swing of a pendulum can be from one extreme to the other. Aggressiveness is now standing on its head, claiming, as it always does, superior rights and a benevolent virtue for having done so. There was a time when sex was not tolerated at all in polite circles, when ladies were not allowed to possess ankles because of their impolite association with the continuity of legs. Progress, however, is not long to be thus restrained, and sexual repression is now replaced by a newer moral code, hallmarked this time as 'science' and named Psycho-analysis. Instead of there being no sex, now everything is sex and to this exalted deity all must bow. (In Russia we have recently seen the elimination of God, with mechanization and the tractor to assume the highest throne in His exalted place; but in our more civilized community there seems to be evidence of a return to a more primitive phallic dictatorship.) In this new Church there is to be no repression and all aspects of the unseen are to be thrown into the light, in order that again there may be a sense of perfect unity within the perfect mind, when psycho-analysed.

AGGRESSIVENESS

Thus to some, sex is not only the cause, it is also the goal of life. It is not only the symptom, it is also the cure, and every aspect of experience is merely some substitution for, or repression of, the fundamental fact of sex, rampant or dormant. We can either escape from sex or into it, and either way can find equally well our method of escape. Masturbation or free love, sensuality and superficiality, in turn offer to our anxiety the protection of the immediate and the seen, against the danger of that intolerable unseen which must play its part in any vital relationship. They each share that same false freedom of timelessness and absoluteness, which is the assumed privilege of those who have successfully eliminated the other pole of their spaciotemporal relationship. The strain of being in a community, related male and female, seems more than many of us can bear, without a bias to one side or the other. We must escape either in this way or that from the process of relationship, and somehow justify the fact that we have done so.

It is curious how morality comes in on either side of narrowmindedness, whether described as 'I ought' or 'I ought not'. Libertinism, being based upon the attitude: 'You ought to set me free,' is just as highly moralized as the falsest Puritanism. According to this new Science, which can no more stand alone without morality than can the Church which it despises, one woman is not enough for one man, because, forsooth: 'I ought to be free to experiment; I ought to have every opportunity for experience that life can bestow; I ought . . .'; and so this moral obsession in favour of self-expression, without the discipline of accepted fact, pro-

146

ceeds to justify the satisfaction of immediate desire.

This way or that way, there is not much to be said in preference for one side or the other, because both fulfil the same policy of negativism and escape from responsiveness. 'You ought to set me free!' It is as if we all feel the presence of some persecutor, bullying us, threatening us, pushing us this way and that. Alas for our satisfaction in life, that this our persecutor should be life itself, the true nature of which we are so anxious to avoid. Because we try so hard to escape, we pay the penalty of symptoms, from which we then seek some easy or expensive cure, provided by a benevolent external saviour.

Being in such hot flight from our pursuing enemy, how can we realize that all we are so anxious to avoid contains the cure? Life is the law for our acceptance, but who can stand the strain of life and love it? This acceptance of the reality of things as they are, actively passive, co-operative and reciprocating, as a seed planted in the darkness, operating in the unseen, unconditionally accepting the full measure of experience, is the privilege of the female role. Seeking only to be the servant of that creation of which it is the living image, acting as the reflecting mirror of a deeper light, our single task is faithfully to tend that light within the intellect which, through its illumination, is prepared to see all things and live amongst them.

This word 'amongst' rings with an old-world sound: but it is a stranger to our behaviour, in spite of being such a commonplace word in our vocabulary. We have not yet learnt how to live amongst one another, as lions amongst lambs, peacefully. 'I send you forth as lambs among wolves.' (Luke, x, 3.) But we won't lie down.

It is interesting that the word 'amongst' does not occur in this sense either in the French or German vocabularies. In French there is 'parmi', but it means in a particular sense, e.g. 'amongst others present were the following'. The words required for translation of 'amongst' into French are 'avec', 'entre' or 'contre': and into German, 'in', 'unter', 'bei', 'mit' or 'zusammen'. There is something new, unfamiliar to society, about this word 'amongst'. We have it in our language, but it seems as if we still prefer to live 'for' or 'against' one another. But 'amongst' is the more important word for peace.

Murder

Murder, being the most extreme example of aggressiveness, requires a section to itself. The motive is not so foreign and unknown to us as we might hope, because, although the practice of murder requires some particular kink to make it possible, the psychology of murder is a much more common matter, which should enable us all to have deep sympathy with the murderer. In fact the psychology of murder is very intimately associated with the organization of society itself, as part of the moralizing of aggressiveness in the system of infinite regress.

1. The motive of the murderer may be divided into two aspects, namely, positive (desire for gain) and negative (revenge). The method of the murderer is 'instant elimination of the obstruction'. Thus by some instant and aggressive method, by some sharp sword or sudden shock, the obstruction is eliminated, the gulf

of time and space is overlapped and the objective is immediately achieved. Viewed from this general standpoint, the psychology of murder is seen to include all that murders life, as for example the apprehensiveness of false hopes, the fixation of illusion, the sentimentality of wrong values and the seductive narcosis of phantasy.

2. Murder being a negative process (a kind of regressive aggressiveness) can then proceed along the path of infinite regress. It is very important that, to save his conscience, the murderer should not have to face the penalty of recognizing, either that murder has been committed, or that he is indeed a murderer. The attitude towards life remains the same, however, the undesirable must be eliminated, the obstruction removed and the murderer murdered in order to achieve the desirable result: 'I am not bad, I am good.'

3. So far so good, but having murdered the murderer in oneself, negatively, it still remains possible to murder the external murderer in someone else, positively. Fortunately there are always scapegoats to be blamed, in regard to whom we can add to our moral virtue by insisting that the law should eliminate them as evil-doers, under the externalized responsibility of 'the State' and with the sword of a quite respectable justice.

4. Murder can be still further legitimized by the declaration of war, when in a 'good cause'. Massed murder can then become so praiseworthy in the sight of God and man as to have become a public duty with which all good citizens (encouraged by their wives and mothers) must agree.

5. There is one other complication, which represents the negative aspect of such legitimized aggressiveness.

Namely, there is a form of 'pacifism' which has been developed out of murdering the desire to kill. Now there must be no hatred, we must be all one, in love. But alas, this state of peace has been arrived at through murdering the lust for war, as will be proved in time of crisis when such pacifists become the most ardent fighters, in order to prove the nobility and selflessness of their pacifist intentions.

The task of sorting out these many types of pacifists according to their many motives may seem impossible, but the thread of an infinite regress will be found to connect many who are most anxious to establish their unselfish innocence. In general, *morality is murder if it is aggressive in regard to truth.* There is no murder in accepted reality, even though it may only be a beloved enemy. But the false equation of 'ought' with 'is', spells MURDER even of that which is life.

An Acquisitive Society

Our leaders are all 'fixers' nowadays. We have many politicians, but no statesmen. The organization of society is no longer in the hands of saints or wise men (who would be four-dimensional), but belongs to those more three-dimensionally minded, whose partiality seeks for tangible proofs of security and privilege. Nowadays we are not 'being': therefore we must have and do. But an acquisitive society is both an aggressive and a sick society. Negative, aggressive and destructive, yet fearing death, it pre-arranges the circumstances of its own funeral and is pre-fixed with the inexorable nature of all that it is most anxious to avoid. Speaking in large capitals of sanctity and rights, honour and glory, it

passes to its inevitable decline in all the mockery of
morals and the panoply of war.

The same principle of fixation is the motive behind
the unreality of its economics. Our god is gold. The
banks, with the gold that they contain, form the sancti-
monious edifice of our modern Church, with banker-
parsons and economist-theologians at its altar, bolster-
ing up this false religion under the name of Capitalism.
Yet the opposite alternative would be no better; for
surely this religion would be just as false if, as religions
can do, it stood upon its head and called itself Communism or Socialism.

There is no salvation in such turning upside down,
nor by adopting another set of equally aggressive
labels. Conversion turns, not upside down nor inside
out, but rather quietly through a right angle, as if it
has been multiplied by that magic symbol of the unseen, the square root of minus one. Yet that is an unnecessarily difficult way of explaining this process,
which involves nothing more complicated or difficult
than the acceptance of both sides, under whatever bilateral classification we may choose, or with which we
may be presented. Ups and downs, rights and wrongs,
lefts and rights, all classifications are possible, and
ranking may be rude upon any scale. We are left, however, when all is said and done, with no real alternative
beyond that of accepting all that comes our way, seen
or unseen, if we are to experience and discover the
universal truth that all are deeply one.

The Adventure of Life

The prerogative of the realist is movement, danger

and adventure. The self-defensive egotist, however, must run away by flight or fight, to fix somehow the strain of a suspense he cannot bear. If we have by now become accustomed to the need for paradox, it will not strike us as so strange that the true adventure of life is that which our war-makers cannot either understand or tolerate. Because life is an adventure, they would fix it to their advantage, since they cannot face the risk of a change which might involve them in some temporary discomfort. Yet whose is the way of adventure today? Perhaps the saddest thought of all in considering this problem of peace and war, is that the whole prerogative of adventure seems to have gone over to the war-makers. To live in truth, which is suspense, *is* adventure, movement, growth, uncertainty, risk and danger. Yet there is little opportunity in life today for experiencing that adventure, unless we go to war. The cowards in us have moralized a fixed, aggressive system, eliminating if possible all adventure as intolerable uncertainty. We are left in this acquisitive society, with youth longing for opportunity, but finding little except in the uncertain path of crime or in the danger of pursuing new records at excessive speed. We have got ourselves into this mess because of our refusal to accept adventure, and now our best adventurers can only find employment in killing one another, and themselves.

We cannot live for ever, and the unseen must in time overwhelm the seen. Death is but rebirth seen on its other face, so that it is not the dying or the dead that matter. There is no solution of our problem to be found in the defensive sanctifications of human life ap-

DIAGRAM 15

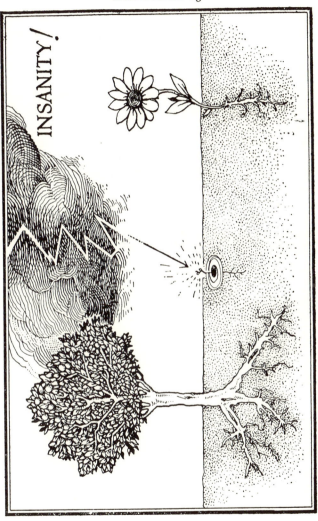

plied by a false humanism. To regard death as a bad thing, to be avoided at all costs, is but another example of our egoistic error. For death is not so evil as the flight from death, which is our present public putrefaction in the morass of infinite regress.

Life is adventure, perhaps for us more truly now than it has ever been. If danger is the hallmark of adventure, Diagram 15 pictures the extent of it. We are so small a seed, the threatening thunder roars with overwhelming voice, the lightning flashes as if directed punitively straight at us. How can so small a seed withstand so great a force? How can so much anxiety and suspense be stretched across so small a frame? The title of the picture is 'Insanity!', for hope itself would seem insane.

Yet courage knows the answer, which is formidable truth. The lightning flash is power escaped that belongs inside the seed. In fact these two forces, apparently at war, are images of one another, and continuous. The seed must say and feel 'I am that'; and absorb it again, accepting a relationship, as tree and flower do, with unlimited eternity.

CHAPTER IV: GUILT

SUMMARY

Dreams.

The Hope of Unity. False identifications; the Church and self-defence; moralized egotism.

Moral Assumptions. 'Conative' and 'cognitive' thinking; the offensive 'ought'; burglar and policeman; errors of idealism.

Guilt. Is not conscience; definitions; the useful scapegoat; the Time factor; the reality of guilt.

Genesis. The tree of knowledge; why the sin? The meaning of temptation; the reality of punishment.

Ecstasy. The uprising dragon; to be as God; return to earth.

Guilt and Sex. Aggressiveness in the nursery; the fear of life; the meaning of masturbation; its equivalents; serpent power and Holy Spirit; encouragement.

Projection. Resistance; escape; the geni and the bottle.

Reality. Metaphysics; attitude; balance; paranoia; the fallacy of all Messiahs.

Confession and Atonement. The satisfaction of being caught; over-indulgence; disgorgement; the last ditch.

CHAPTER IV: GUILT
DREAMS[1]

VII. 'The Garden of Eden'

I was walking down hill along a country road with two girl friends. It was a very lovely day, everything most attractive: we stopped under a tree which bore the most beautiful fruit. They seemed to be peaches but were pear-shaped, shining golden, with a lovely flush on them. I wanted to gather them at once, but the others said it would be wrong. However, I over-ruled their objections and gathered a huge bundle of the fruit which I tied up in my mackintosh. The other girls gathered a few also.

Then a very handsome man came along, wearing the uniform of the North West Frontier Mounted Police, and began talking to us in a very friendly way. He told us how some people who came along that road were in the habit of stealing the fruit, and did not seem to notice what we had done. We did not tell him, but after a while I realized that he had really known all the time. He then said he must see what was inside our bundles and when he discovered the fruit he gave us a great telling off. The other girls were furious with me for getting them into trouble.

Then it was evening and with another two girls I was fixing up an appointment to go dancing. When we got there we saw the others dancing but we were not allowed to join in, at which I felt extremely dis-appointed. It was a curious, sleepy sort of dance, mysterious under shaded light, and I felt very un-happy.

[1] For comment, see Appendix (page 306).

156

DREAMS

VIII. 'Woolworths'

I was walking by the sea-shore, when I noticed some flowers growing in a cottage garden. 'How awful!' I thought, 'they are synthetic.'

Chapter IV

GUILT

The Hope of Unity

Whatever may be the truth about the 'Absolute' in 'Eternity', the Space-Time world in which we live is a duality. This implies an obligation upon each one of us to move in some relationship. Life and circumstance have their laws which, as it were, speak for themselves for us to listen to if we so choose. But we have the illusion of freewill which enables us to argue and even to 'beat time' for a while if we feel disposed, with added sense of virtue for so doing.

This aggressiveness of choice not only asserts the rights and privileges of another time, but also of another relationship. The infamous 'ought' demands that there should be not two but one, not 'the time' or your time, but my time or no time, and there is never any doubt which one is meant. Some of these innumerable manifestations under which aggressiveness may the more aggressively cover itself, have been referred to in the previous chapter.

This idea that we ought to be one, unfortunately draws encouragement from many different experiences. It is the happy state of 'infinite' and indivisible relationship between mother and child *in utero*, which

159

all of us once knew. It is for this reason that the condition of the child in the womb is taken as the primary
pattern of all neurotic desire and discontent, because
of the regressive desire to fix the 'as you were'; so that
the labels Nirvana, womb, child, Heaven and neurotic, have come to possess a largely rude significance.
There is nothing wrong, however, with Heaven, mothers or children. The only wrongness is to adopt a defensive policy of fixation, in a world which demands a
more positive acceptance of its movement.

This fixed identity of self within benevolent circumstance, typified by the child-mother relationship, is,
however, a pinnacle of experience which some people,
possessed of positions of assured security and privilege,
can count amongst their natural assets. Fortunate circumstances of birth, which combine both wealth and
opportunity for these select few, convey the impression
that in order to be like them we ought also to live in
circumstances which offer the best possible chance to
our important selves. If for some the best is right, why
not for all? Thus the privileged classes may go through
life from nursery to grave with their sense of privilege
unbroken, although in different circumstances they
might prove incapable of facing sterner facts. They
have good reason, therefore, for retaining a strong
moral sense that things always ought to be just so,
fixed for their advantage. In fact we may feel sure that
any classification into 'haves' and 'have nots' is backed
on both sides by this worthy 'ought'; one side 'ought to
have' and is quite sure that those others 'ought not to
have', which is exactly the impression of the other party,
but expressed the other way round. There is so much

wealth, opportunity and privilege; and yet it is not safe
to assume that anyone ought to have such great advantages, or that we ought to have things all our own
way, or be left in private and secure possession of gains
which we have never earned.

What is quite certain is that, being in possession of
our property (however we or our fortunate but not
always scrupulous ancestors may have obtained it), we
shall then turn policeman in our moral disapproval of
anyone who threatens to take it away from us. This is
what has happened to all private estates, however
come by, and in fact to the British Empire as a whole.
Even the Archbishop of Canterbury has granted the
imperial policeman full rights to protect the one-time
burglar's swag. At a Diocesan conference at Canterbury he was reported as saying: 'The force of an army
used for the defence of the people was right. . . . That
defence went a long way, and in the case of this
country it would include not only the defence of terri-
tory, of the homes and lives of the people, but those
trade routes on whose freedom the subsistence of the
people depended. . . . The use of force, of the sword
by the State, was the ministry of God for the protection of the people. If the force of an army were used
for national aggression or acquisition or self-assertion
it was wrong. If it were used for the defence of the
people it was right.'

If, however, we are looking fairly at those deeper
causes of unrest which operate from the unseen, we
cannot take so naïve a view as to regard the policeman
as always justified in maintaining the fixation of a false
security. A little imperial egotism is all very well, but

it can go too far when burglar and policeman, Church and State, are all agreed that the only thing they want is assured security, in which to enjoy their dubious gains. Such an attitude towards life must be largely spent in the accusative, with the inevitable result of war, either defensive or offensive.

Egotism is doubly awkward in its relationships, because we can so easily become identified with whatever we would regard as most precious. When this process has taken place, we are as anxious that the beloved should be possessed of a place in the sun as that we should occupy one ourselves. The process of egotistic self-extension swells to the Committee of which we are even a lesser member, and soon includes the honour of our beloved country. But we have become none the less selfish for that degree of egotistic self-extension.

The process of identification also operates when the self becomes attached not only to one but also to many aspects of its circumstance. Identified with its audience and seeing it in so many forms, the self becomes in the position of a watcher over Piccadilly Circus, determined to protect every item of the traffic in whatever direction it may move. Such is the position in which the pacifist is liable to find himself, as he watches over the multiplicity of movements in rapacious and anxious Europe. Morally attached in all directions and with interfering finger more active than observant eye, our pacifists become involved in all directions in someone else's war.

This false identification is very easily confused with sympathy, thus reaping an undue reward. Yet it is not the same thing, for the important reason that in true sympathy there is an inter-polarity, an abyss of actual negative, which stands between and separates self and not-self, this and that. There may be much sympathy between mother and child; but this sympathy should never be allowed to be confused with an identity, which robs relationship of the pain of being a duality in fact, making of it only a unity in phantasy. 'I am not you' is the only just protection, when it comes to an argument with egotism. There will be less confusion, however, if we agree to use the word 'compassion' to take the place of more doubtful sympathy, but in that virtue there must not be the same error of identification. Compassion we may be allowed if we give it the true meaning of 'suffering with'; but sympathy is often more misused because of the false identification which it so readily assumes, as the secure means of escape from a state of tension which is the proof of life. The fact is that we are always two, but by one means or another we shall forget it while we can.

Moral Assumptions

Unfortunately, there is much that is cast within the pattern of the human mind itself, that makes it easy for us to fall into the trap of omnipotent interference. It is so easy to think we can, and thus to think we ought, in spite of outward evidence to the contrary.

In Diagram 16 (a), Reality is shown by the relationship of self in circumstance, where these two are shaded to show their difference, polarized to one another as positive (inner) and negative (outer). In Diagram 16 (b), however, the shading covers both self and circum-

DIAGRAM 16

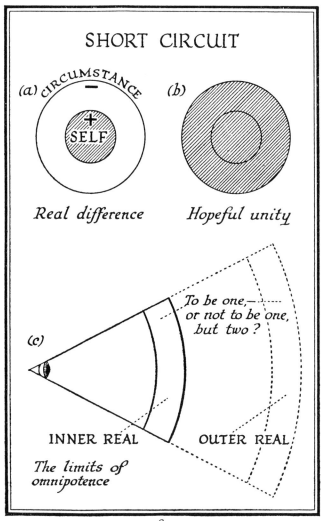

SHORT CIRCUIT

(a) CIRCUMSTANCE — SELF +

Real difference

(b)

Hopeful unity

(c) To be one,—
or not to be one,
but two ?

INNER REAL   OUTER REAL

*The limits of
omnipotence*

stance, to show that false identification has created a false unity. In Diagram 16 (c), the same situation is illustrated slightly differently, the 'self' including both the eye of the observer and the mental screen upon which movements of the mind take place (i.e. consciousness). Within this private universe the self is omnipotent, to create as it may choose, and to draw its own pictures according to its own most desirable phantasy. Within our minds we can believe anything, until we are forced to check up between our private inner universe and that more public outer one in which we live. But Reality remains a law outside ourselves. Unfortunately, however, we need seldom conform to it, owing to this liberty which we have within ourselves to make more egotistic choice, according to our taste.

This diagram may therefore be taken to illustrate what was defined in Chapter I as 'conative' thinking, which was there contrasted with the truer and rarer 'cognitive' thinking. Conative thinking insists upon an equation between our inner or private universe and the outer world. It chooses as far as it can an outer world to coincide with the world of inward choice. Cognitive thinking, on the other hand, is not thus bent on egotistic interference, but uses the world of sense and consciousness only to act as observant mediator between the self and the circumstances in which it lives and moves. It is obvious that conative thinking is going to attempt to impose a pattern of aggressive interference upon external reality, whether this be a child or some larger society upon which interference can aggressively operate.

It is important to realize how this aggressiveness

will always be moralized by means of an offensive 'ought'. The pattern which we can create within our own minds and our private universe, being omnipotent, seems to be boundlessly 'good', and it therefore seems as if that outer world should also conform happily to this inward ideal pattern. Since this within myself is so much better than that outside, it should be obvious to everybody, besides myself, that all that which is outside should be as good as this within me. Unfortunately, such moralizing is based upon a false assumption, but false premises make the best foundation for a 'good' war. It does seem, however, that people of active minds, who are most quick to see advantages and opportunities, are those who, unless they are careful, are going to attempt to force their own quicker time upon the slower time in which they live. Quickness of mind may lead to intolerance, and intellectual advantage is itself one of the subtler seeds of war, especially between adult and child. But our 'times' are aspects of our very 'selves', and thus are different and deserving each of its own respect.

The truth is that the mental screen of consciousness, within our own private universe of mind, is not at all to be regarded as a privileged autocrat, but rather in fact as the servant of two masters, both unseen; namely, the worlds of inward and outward reality respectively. This 'ME' is the referee or mediator between two moving systems, both growing and changing, and both constantly subject to a multiplicity of moving relationships. However much Me would like to think so, Me is not the only one, and that perhaps is why Me is inclined to insist upon a more important role of

mastery and privilege. Dictators are always to be suspect, whether they are dictators of an inward private
world, or of a larger outward state.

It is so easy to deceive ourselves in many different
ways. Egotism may behave as a plain burglar, ad-
dicted to stealing and lying as a means of ensuring
privilege, and thus plainly showing criminal propensi-
ties. But although such manifestations of minor crime
are greeted with heavy punishment on the part of an
aggressively defensive society, it is more right to assume that they are only an exhibition of an anxiety
state, defending itself against the uncertainty of an
intolerable suspense. A more complicated (and more
common?) method of self-ensuring privilege, however,
is to be found in the habits of more highly coloured
burglars. Dreamers, phantasists, idealists or politicians,
they have created within their own minds an exalted
system which, because of its superiority, they are anxious to foist upon a less enlightened community which
they feel sure is in need of salvation at their hands.
Such burglary does not meet with social disapproval
and is very liable to succeed in winning the major advantage, through attaining the best of both worlds. In
fact such moral exaltation can reach the highest degrees of uplift and approval, and can be rewarded
by important positions of responsibility in State and
Church. Assuming these responsibilities, these morally
successful ones then cover the whole community with
embarrassment and shame, involving them in wars,
which can never be good for anyone.

The false assumption upon which such idealism is
based is that it is our duty to force moral phantasy

upon more actual fact. The argument can be speciously defended, and always looks good to those who are anxious to defend the security of privilege.

When the Archbishop of Canterbury (see page 161), (and the Archbishop of York has at times made similar utterances), can himself speak with such moral persuasion in favour of the rights and virtues of war, it should make us suspect that we have to look further than the Evil One for the source of our troubles. The point has already been emphasized that our enemy is not in 'evil', but in masquerading 'goodness'. Let us therefore examine in more detail the method of this exalted self-righteousness, in which moral egotism is preserved in absolute security, fixity and peace. Such a condition of unchanging moral superiority is obviously worth most to a defensive egotist, and is going to be defended ardently against attack. We might say that such a position would be of 'priceless' value, but unfortunately there always is a price, even if it has to be paid by someone else.

The tyranny of self-righteous interference is of such unquestionable advantage that everyone feels he wants to have his turn at King of the Castle. Unfortunately, however, there are many other 'dirty rascals', who have to be aggressively eliminated when they come to ask for their share of these desirable spoils. In order to preserve the stability of society under such conditions, everybody has to be offered something to their apparent advantage, as sops to Cerberus. This may take the form of the encouragement of moral virtues, such as the advantages of humility and poverty or of alcohol, to which in the sacred name of freedom everyone should be allowed access, if only in order to drown their sorrows so that they may thus remain as unquestioned Kings of the Castle within their own phantasy. Cinemas, novels, and every kind of 'dope' also have the same effect of making the dispossessed feel better, each within the illusion of his own private universe. Such dwellers in phantasy, however, are always liable to the penalty of disillusion, and it is sometimes difficult to persuade the dispossessed of the higher virtue of their position, when others are dwelling in palaces of more obvious material advantage. The time will come when the pendulum will swing, and a false relationship will pay the penalty of revolution.

Who can believe in the Church of to-day? Whatever light may come from the world of the Spirit, it is but rarely shown in the public pronouncements of ecclesiastical dignitaries. There has never been a time when the clear enlightenment of larger values was more required, but it is no use looking to the Churches for that deep aid. They seem to have got stuck in the moral ditches of their own self-righteousness, which they are defending against all comers, certain of their virtue despite their apprehensive and aggressive errors. 'King of the Castle' has become the Church's game, and the ecclesiastical God seems to have no greater virtue than that of any other dirty rascal.

However, it is quite possible to play this game successfully, and there are many different variations of it which can be worked in turn, in order to preserve an unsmudged and unbroken shell of moral equanimity. The human mind is very contagious in its capacity to spread infection. It is very plastic in suggestibility, and will readily change from the worship of a painted idol to that of a mechanical tractor, if it is sure that it is going to get immediate advantage and security thereby. But there is one inward enemy who is not so easily eliminated and which, when once it is aroused, is the cause of endless discomfort to the marauding and fearful self. When the systematized versions of privilege fail to be convincing to our moral sense, we have to face the discomforts of this thing called Guilt. What is it, and what does it mean?

Guilt

The first thing to realize about Guilt is that it is quite possible to be guilty and not feel guilty, or conversely to feel guilty and not to be guilty. Again we must be warned against the meaningless concept of unchanging absolutes, for all things change according to the nature of our relationship towards them. For the truth of this, as indeed of all other matters, is that it is not 'it', but our attitude towards 'it', that counts.

We can be guilty, but we can successfully and agressively eliminate our guilt. If this method is to be successful, however, it must be employed continuously and unswervingly and the process of elimination must be pursued hot foot: e.g. (1) I am not guilty, (2) Indeed (to make sure) I am quite perfect, (3) In fact it is obviously you who are guilty, (4) Therefore you must be punished by elimination. This is a perfect system, and cannot go wrong as long as it is carried out with sufficient perseverance and unswerving pertinacity. But as soon as there is any kind of break, the other extreme of guilt unsatisfied is liable to be set in operation. Whilst successful, however, it is important to notice that the system is continually destructive, and that it must have some kind of scapegoat. It is usually not difficult to find the necessary 'dirty rascal' for due punishment, but somewhere there must always be a vacant neck to keep the axe busy. For reasons which are not entirely alien to their own psychology, it has been the especial privilege of Jews in history to occupy this unenviable position of the necessary scapegoat.

What then is Guilt? For definition, let us suggest the following: 'Guilt is a feeling caused by some unlawful acquisition or falsification of fact, in which desire has been gratified either presumptuously or prematurely.' In terms of time and balance, realizing that there is this inward truth which is the very nature and foundation of all reality, we feel ourselves 'off balance' if we have made a false step either in space or time. Guilt is that feeling of inward pause which would pull us back to true.

It is necessary at this point to distinguish between Guilt and Conscience, because these again (like intuition and instinct, feeling and emotion) are not to be regarded as synonyms, but as opposites. Conscience can be classed with Instinct and Emotion, Guilt—with its deeper measure of reality to which we have referred —with Intuition and Feeling. In other words, conscience is what we do in self-defence about our guilt and it expresses our attitude towards, or feeling about, guilt. Guilt may be aggressively eliminated by the successful bounder who has no conscience, or it may be unsuccessfully eliminated by the melancholic, whose complaint is not so much 'I am guilty', as 'Alas! I ought not to be guilty'.

If we are honest with ourselves we know that it is quite possible to be guilty but happy. Our guilt in fact is truth: and if we are to be real in our attitude towards life, it would be as well to plead guilty and also to be happy. (Sinner, yes: but miserable, no.) Living as we do, it is extremely difficult not to be guilty in some way; but if it is so much a fundamental necessity in life to be our own egotistic selves in spite of others, there is no need to be so miserably attached to a self-defensive conscience about it. 'Yes, I am guilty' is the feeling of a fearful heart, which nevertheless is prepared to face the inevitable punishment which must be meted out in time. Conscience, however, is a miserable attempt aggressively to eliminate the stain upon the shield, as if the fact that it ought not to be there means that it is any the less. Better to say 'Yes, I am guilty, and I am willing to realize that life itself is part of such a strain'. We are brought up in the end by this analysis, in accordance with common sense. It is the deepest light which theology can shed upon the problems of our living, but unfortunately the defensive-moralistic attitude of a neurotic church has almost entirely obscured it from the ways of men.

Guilt from Genesis

It is possible to deduce any theory that we like from dreams, and to interpret such flimsy metaphors in any way that takes our fancy. It is the very nature of symbolism that it is the most plastic and fruitful of mediums for the manipulation of our minds, but no one can say whether the interpretation which we choose to give is true or not. The ancient myths of biblical tradition have been exploited *ad infinitum*, and the commentaries written upon the deeper wisdom of mankind are usually only successful in obscuring their light. The symbolism of dreams, however, being just of this plastic kind, offers immense possibilities. It is very interesting to see how the symbolism of the Garden of Eden story constantly recurs not only in other religious myths, but also in our dreams. The Tree and the Garden, the Serpent and the Apple, the Woman and the Man, illustrate the story of our lives. (See the dream 'Garden of Eden', quoted at the beginning of this chapter, as an example.)

In the following quotation from the story of Adam and Eve in Genesis, let us interpret the garden as the psyche, Adam and Eve as the male and female aspects of the self, the tree as growth in time, the serpent as the life force (experienced as desire), and the fruit as achievement in the external world of consciousness. The whole story may then be read as if it illustrates the problem of aggressiveness in terms of time. Temptation is impatience, sin is achievement out of time, guilt is awareness of our error, death is the pain inherent in rebirth, and punishment is but the justice of redress. But let us see.

In the first chapter of Genesis we read: 'He planted the Tree of Life also in the midst of the garden, and the Tree of Knowledge of good and evil.'

God: 'Of every tree of the Garden thou mayest freely eat, but of the tree of the knowledge of good and evil thou shalt not eat, for in the day thou eatest thereof thou shalt surely die.'

GUILT

Serpent: 'Hath God said ye shall not eat . . .?'

Eve: 'Of the fruit of the tree which is in the midst of the garden, God hath said ye shall not eat it lest ye die.'

Serpent: 'Ye shall be as God, knowing good and evil.'

She ate and gave her husband to eat, and then ashamed, they hid. The voice of God, speaking in the garden in the cool of the evening, said: 'But who told thee?'

Man: 'The woman thou gavest me, she gave me of the tree and I did eat.'

To the woman God said: 'What is this that thou hast done?' And she replied: 'The serpent beguiled me and I did eat.'

Each blamed the other according to the best traditions of external cause, but did not thereby escape due punishment. Then followed enmity 'between thy seed and her seed, between head and heel'; the pangs of creation and the rule of aggressive man; the disappointment of labour, 'thorns and thistles shall it bring forth' . . . 'till thou return unto the ground'.

The interpretation of this story may be evaluated in terms of the time problem, and by means of the familiar diagram of the circle (page 175). The tree in the garden is the Tree of Life and the garden is the larger psyche of the self. The serpent is that which is symbolized in the East as the dragon, the energy of creative desire, speaking through the moment now as 'I want'. (St. George is therefore a very conscientious man.) The woman is the unseen and inner aspect of the creative psyche, fluid and inarticulate, intuitive and direct; the man is the male aspect of the psyche, twice-disciplined

174

DIAGRAM 17

THE TREE IN THE GARDEN

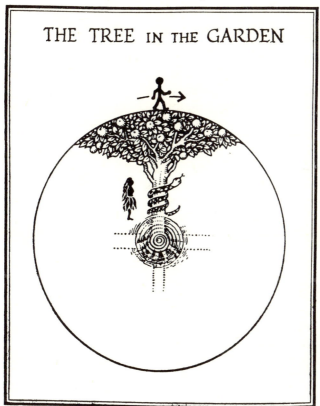

executive, whose task it is to do and have, related both to the inward and external worlds.

If desire is allowed to speak out of turn, obtaining effects before those effects are due, a crime has been committed which is in fact an error in terms of time, a prematurity, an egotistic precocity, an authoritarian insistence upon the rights of self in spite of fact. The reward of such aggressiveness can only be punishment, but this is not to be regarded as an arbitrary or authoritarian activity on the part of some external divine being. It is a most scientific and metaphysical experience of the inevitable law of life. That which is plucked too soon will also fade too soon, falling into the ground there to be again reborn at another time. This is the law of life, to be understood in terms of fact, and not idolized as the interference of some external or so-called divine being. 'Honesty is the best policy'— because: 'The wages of sin is death.' Not, however, that death is so bad a thing, for it must also be rebirth, if we are willing that it should be so. Until we can learn to live abiding by the laws of space and time, we cannot expect to draw the richest harvest from experience.

Aggressiveness even unto death itself is an attitude towards life which can best be expressed by the metaphysical diagnosis of the 'infinite regress'. There are thus two ways even of dying; and two deaths, negative and positive. Acceptance, on the other hand, which is the development of a positive attitude towards experience, an ingratiation of the self into its necessary discipline, fulfils the creative law symbolized in the growth of the tree of life, the mating of female and male to create the child; and makes manifest that uprising of the dragon, which is akin to rising sap or the development in time of the fullest energy which abides within the self. Then death is no longer to be regarded only as a bad thing, a punishment, but can be seen in due proportion as the true fulfilment of the greater

DIAGRAM 18

COMPETITION ᴀɴᴅ CO·OPERATION

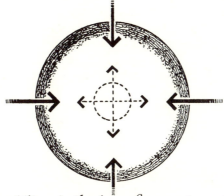

(a)

Competition is the law of crime & conflict

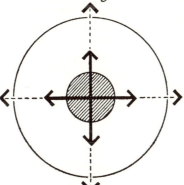

(b)

Co-operation is the law of love

law of life. Only the criminal (impatient one) need fear the punishment of law, and only he who has not learnt to live need fear to die.

The urge of aggressive competition is illustrated in Diagram 18 (a), where the forces within the psyche, or between self and circumstance, are set in opposition one against the other, aggressiveness always being associated with the predominant negative of a destructive attitude towards life. Diagram 18 (b), however, illustrates the law of love working in co-operation from the centre outwards as the sap rising in the tree, or as the development of the serpent force, the uprising dragon, within the self.

Ecstasy

The trouble is, however, that there is so much opportunity for inward experience of this uprising dragon, that we are often able to appreciate some flash of ecstasy which seems to insist upon our immediate communion with the utmost and the highest. We can be as gods within ourselves, experiencing within the limits of our private universe the powers and privileges of the divine being, omnipotent and eternal. This is an easy matter and illustrates for us again the dangers of life within our garden, where the fruit of the tree of the knowledge of good and evil can make us experience the unlimited powers that dwell within the psyche.

This feeling of well-being may be expressed in less theological form in the terms: 'I feel as if I could push a bus over', illustrating the sense of unlimited power within the self. The inward sense of power and worth can rise (especially in adolescence) with so great a feeling of divine immanence as to bring with it the flash of instantaneous conversion. . . . 'God is so much in me that I feel as if I really am one with God.' Those who feel such ecstasy, however, should not be listed as fresh subjects for theological incarceration, because it is in fact only a state of ecstatic escape from the reality of the soul's incarnation within the difficulties of space and time. Ecstasy is all very well; but for us it belongs within the limits of space and time, which means that it must come down to earth again, there to be expressed in terms of toil and labour, suffering and disappointment (Diagram 19, page 180). The light of instantaneous conversion must be brought down to the shadows of our space-time world in the lantern of our body-mind, and our experience of God is to be patiently expressed within the limitations of awkward relationship in an egotistic and impatient community.

Diagram 19 illustrates this easy ecstasy, which dreams frequently describe as ascending in a lift, or flying on unbounded wings through unlimited air. A little of it goes a very long way, but the law is that it should be brought back to earth again, expressed in space and time, accepted through the discipline of our technique of living.

As another example of the reality of experience within the 'fourth dimension', the ecstasy of sexual intercourse is also to be regarded as subject to this same discipline. The same law applies, and it should not be regarded as some absolute and separated desirable experience, but rather as an experience the value of which depends upon our capacity to bring it down to earth, expressing it in everyday life, to work its way

DIAGRAM 19

ECSTASY

**Bring it down to earth again:
this flight is too easy**

amidst the larger tasks of love. Ecstasy, whether
mystical or sexual, is not to be reserved for isolated
opportunity, but to be expressed in common-sense
experience, every day and in every way. This does not
mean that ecstasy is to be avoided, but that it should
be allowed its place in full relationship with every

other form and limitation of human experience. As a sexual experience, it is one of the deepest aspects of the profound nature of rhythm in life. It is a function of time itself, and therefore in most need of being timely, if it is to avoid the penalty of guilt.

Sex

There cannot be much peace in any place where sex is blamed as sin, for this is the root conflict of all aggressive bias. It teaches a false attitude towards life: up with good, and down with evil which is a bad thing to be destroyed. Yet how can sex be sin, if it is the true function of duality in relationship? The labels have become reversed, for sin is not in sex, but in the refusal to be thus intimately fired by the stimulus of a relationship. The truth of sin is to be 'unsectioned', unweaned: only a false morality could commit this deepest crime of blaming sex as root of evil. If blame there is to be, then these moralists must blame not sex, but life itself, for their discomfiture.

Although to seek for a beginning, as first cause of blame, is no part of our search for truth, yet the seed of much subsequent aggressiveness is sown in nursery morality. This child, as infant, growing, 'is': but aggressiveness, seeing only what is is not, yet ought to be at some later time, imposes a false external pattern, laying down the law: 'Take that!' It is bad to be naughty: so this 'love' (approval for convenience sake) which is conditional and not love at all, demands a standard of behaviour that is untrue to growth at this particular time. Nurses are aggressive with their rewards and punishments, praise and blame. Parents

181

are aggressive, with their urgent hopes and cowardly fears lest hope may once again prove false. There is a mood of thrust and grab in many nurseries, which can only induce a like aggressiveness in children. This is then treated to further aggressiveness by punishment and blame, according to the manner of infinite regress.

But two eyes are better than one for our perspective. Two feet are required for balance, and two hands for sensitive touch. So does the parent and child relationship require to recognize that not either one is right, but two are necessary, even if both are wrong, as probably indeed they are. Meanwhile, if naughtiness exists on either side, there is need for that naughtiness to be expressed and realized. If we are allowed to be ourselves, then we all need to be naughty sometimes, because in fact we are so incomplete, at every age. It is better to be honest and see the truth, even if we do not like it in ourselves, than to hide it for fear of what it means.

We are afraid of all living things, because they move us with messages from the unseen, from which we anxiously escape to the seen and tangible. Children are invisible, intangible, unknown: therefore they must aggressively be boxed and parcelled, fixed and pegged, filled and labelled, so that we may know better that they are 'all right'. Then of course they might still be better than they are: they ought (but is this possible?) each one to be better than every other, and so we reward them for success in competition, awarding marks for 'better', blame and punishment for 'worse'.

From nursery to school aggressiveness continues, driving sheep and goats, dulling the sensitives, urging

182

the insensitives, until all can be successfully numbered amongst the 'saints'. It is not strange that many sinners should fall out, the failures of the system. Nor is it to be wondered at that these, when they come to closer grips with life, should subsequently prove themselves to be the best and most alive.

Both home and school, so sure of sin, so terrified of truth, so anxious to eliminate all enemies, unite together in a conspiracy of silence to smother sex. 'Treat all girls as if they were your sisters!' is the pious advice of parsons who cannot bear that any difference of opinion should exist. Next best to there being no sex, would be if all of us could be sisters! Unfortunately, product of this teaching, too many of us are.

Enemy of all aggressiveness, the bogy of these adolescent years is masturbation. This is the enemy that aggressive virtue, like St. George the Dragon, must successfully eliminate for good. Here much might be said, but it is enough to show the working of the law.

The crimes in regard to which we are most intolerant are those of which we are ourselves most guilty. Therefore a murderous (i.e. eliminative) and masturbating (i.e. timeless, unrelated) generation can have no sympathy with murderers and masturbators. Masturbation is timeless and unrelated physical ecstasy. It is the product, therefore, of a timeless and unrelated technique in education, which first creates it out of error, and then strives punitively to eliminate it by the same means that created it. (All disease is thus an attempt at cure.) But the life force, repressed aggressively at one point, emerges aggressively at another. It is now free to operate as 'religiosity' (spiritual masturbation), or as aggressive interference with the liberties of others for their good (moral masturbation), or as pursuit of knowledge (mental masturbation), in each case compulsively, timelessly and aggressively unrelated. These virtues escape punishment, as of course they would in a community which is only anxious to escape the point of truth.

In masturbation, both as regards its oppressors and its substitutes, the motive is possessed of all the aggressive simplicity of a short-cut through facts. Whether physical or mental, individual or collective, domestic or national, the label of 'masturbation' aptly refers to every attempt to exploit a situation to egotistic advantage, without the discipline of acceptance of the inner and outer world of living and moving facts. It is always timeless and aggressive. It is a crime of impatience that 'must-have now' and will not let well (or ill) alone. It is anxious, arbitrary and egotistic, and its bad manners have no respect either for living facts or living people. It is a way of war, this omnipotent and ecstatic habit of untimely dictatorship.

Impatience cannot let ill alone, and thus, since ill is itself a product of the vicious circle of impatient enterprise, the good work goes on. Feeling that the devil himself is after me, I feel that I must chase after you, even though I loudly claim that I come only as a moral missionary for the good of your immortal soul. The scapegoat is always the needed outward balance of the over-enthusiastic moral missionary, who holds himself up and keeps himself going by having someone to convert and something to do about the error of someone else's ways. Such is the opportunity of nurses and parents, parsons and politicians; which perhaps explains our lack of progress in the art of living in a community.

There are times in our lives when the 'Serpent Power', inward source of growth developing within the self, sets free new flowerings of energy, to be used to our advantage or disadvantage. Adolescence, in particular, is one of such periods, when the 'Serpent Power' is expressed in a new release of energy, which may be directed either into physical, intellectual or religious-emotional channels. Because our parents, teachers and parsons have all been taught to be afraid of this Serpent and also of its power, the tendency in either case will be for this energy to be defensively misdirected into egotistic channels, and somehow fixed in safe detachment from life. It seems too dangerous to leave this force free to find its larger discipline of relationship in movement and experience.

The first idea of self-defence is always to 'cut it out'. It is not altogether unfair to see our elders and betters playing that nursery game of Oranges and Lemons with us, as in our youth we are chased helter-skelter, timelessly urged down the corridors of time. Chop-chop-chop-chop-chop-CHOP: oranges or lemons? Between such harmless alternatives we are made to live, pulling hither and thither in unimportant strife, hoping thus to avoid the deeper reality of conflict. There seems to be so much cowardice in our mentors at this time. They seek to eliminate the serpent altogether, sacking boys for masturbation, cramming them with 'work', tiring them with 'play', or acquiring their immortal scalps for Christianity at the unbalanced moment of emotion and ecstasy. Why are we so frightened by the uprising Dragon? We are afraid of youth: we are afraid of Life. The fear may be true enough to fact, but it is not good for us or them that our teachers should so virtuously run away.

The unseen other aspect of this untimely error of masturbation is the Holy Spirit, source of communion, deepest ecstasy, but opposite pole. To interfere with one is to upset the other, to which the lower needs in time to be lovingly lifted. As it becomes fitly spaced in time, it works its way in body, mind and spirit, for the fulfilment of life's promise.

Of course we cannot cut life out of life. We can only block one channel, for the flow to find another as inferior substitute. There cannot be any doubt that it is fear that causes overwork at school; fear of what might happen, if there were more space of leisure for life to fill. Organized play is liable to become a tedium of righteous effort, in the dubious belief that boys are safer if tired out. Safer from what? From themselves? Much of their class-work is not for their greater culture, but has the purpose of a cul-de-sac, into which they are driven out of unseen fear, for safety's sake. Religion is the most dangerous of all channels of escape for adolescence, because it will either fix successfully this uprushing immaturity, or it will itself be burst, to be useless subsequently because over-exercised too soon.

We cannot cut out this life force. We can only misdirect it, thus focusing too much attention on certain aspects of life, at the expense of neglecting others. Flight from fear is no motive for our living. It is the motive of infinite regress and should not be the prime mover of the vast organization of our educational system. If it is so, then thus it sows the seeds of war. The alternative is that encouragement should take the place of all aggressiveness, so that we each may live in positive acceptance, not only of what we are, but also of our circumstances.

It is characteristic of adolescence that there may be this alternative flowering of interest, either into religion, intellect or sex. In any one of these three, the flowering may be a premature and precocious communion with God, where our Little Jack Horner sits in a corner pulling out plums and feeling good. The experience of guilt which such a pious practice subsequently engenders, however, will be inclined to force the adolescent towards still more precocious heights of religious experience, using this pathway of infinite regress as an escape from fearful truth. Our attitude towards all such high flyers, whether sexual, intellectual or religious should be exactly the same. We should bring them down to earth and there encourage them to fit into the limitations of space and time. Not that they would thereby lose their light, however, but use it more simply for domestic purposes.

Salvation comes not by Messiahs, but from relationship. Adolescence should see the end of Absolutes, as we experience another weaning from that which has previously seemed 'good'. Not 'I' but 'Us'; and Yes to both, which must include our dragon too, who is the seed of life and light bringer within us. St. George needs holding off at this critical time, because he does not understand, not having yet experienced the greater love which proves the unity of all.

GUILT

Conflict, both inner and outer; hysteria and paranoia; internal or external war, are all bred by such
simple domestic misunderstanding of the way of life.
There are so many cases of disguised domestic parasi-
tism, where mothers exploit the 'Deeper Purpose' and
the 'Higher Cause', seeking to enforce their own most
virtuous discoveries of convenient methods of salvation
at the wrong time and in the wrong manner upon
developing children, thus leading to conflict later in
that child. Restless because thus overburdened by a
salvation that was not his own, perhaps this child may
grow up to 'need' politics in deadly earnest to sustain
him. Then his same inward conflict may find itself
again externalized, as nation locks nation in the vice of
aggressive misunderstanding. In some nursery of the
past, national disasters have thus been created to take
their place in history. Our future, for better or worse,
is being planned with fatal force in the nurseries of
to-day.

The causes of war are distant, multiple, confused.
Yet popular fallacy prefers the simple error of attri-
buting the significance of 'cause' to some external epi-
sode, implying fault where fact would do as well. It is
this attitude towards life, when carried into politics,
that breeds war. Unfortunately, however, it is so generally accepted and emphasized, that the ignorant and
inwardly maladjusted majority will always be inclined
to preach the same gospel of external aggressive interference. As we were taught when young, so shall we
teach when grown up. Whether it is from our exalted
desks as teachers in school, or from our pens as pundits
of the Press, or from our castellated pulpits, these same

doctrines of insistence upon war will be promulgated.

Projection

There is good cause, however, that there should be so much resistance from the thin skin of consciousness to these deeper forces which dwell within us. Whether the symbolism is that of snake or serpent, or of some lesser seed of power, we are wise to regard with suspicion these latent forces that hold us so freely and uncertainly in suspense. They need some holding in or down, and there is no doubt that in all of us there is a strong and necessary resistance towards these deeper psychic emanations. Formed rather precariously upon the surface of experience, it is as if we feel within ourselves some hidden danger, some deep sense of strain, which threatens to disturb our sense of self and peace of mind.

Challenged by this deep inward pressure from the unseen, the normal process would be to find suitable channels for its expression, that thus the sap might rise and bring forth fruit in due season. Such patience seems to be beyond us, however, for there is so much more to do than wait. For instance, we can effect some swifter change upon the surface of events, aggressively eliminating this inward enemy from the field of action altogether. Or so it seems, although in fact he is not so easily hidden, because the law of balance must always be maintained.

Since we are thus at war within ourselves, the same pattern is then also copied externally. The enemy is both within and without our gates, for we have put him there by this effort to get rid of him. The psychic force or serpent power, seed of so much potential virtue, having once been thus rejected as evil, is then externalized, and that force which belongs within the self becomes its outward enemy, potential persecutor. The next step in our process of hopeful make-believe is to give our 'Daemon' (now demon) or 'Genius' (now geni) a handy form of symbolism, by which we may control him, as by calling upon a word. He may be God or Devil (and must indeed be both), for privilege and placation. But politics are also derived from this same world of reality displaced, so that this new man-made Messiah may well have a most earthly message to dictate, as he assumes the highest role of nation's God, too-welcome Saviour of all those who have been oppressed. Born of so much misunderstanding, child of repression and escape from fact, his dubious ancestry leaves little doubt that this Messiah will hardly be a Prince of Peace.

Reality

What then is the true nature of this external world in which we live? To find the truth, we are again engaged in metaphysical abstractions. Has it a reality of its own, objective, independent—or is it to be regarded only as the image of ourselves? Are we to say 'I am that', or 'I am Not that', or perhaps both?

Certainly it is true that our attitude towards this 'real' external world is determined by our attitude towards these forces which exist within ourselves. It is as if in that outer world we are seeing ourselves as within a mirror. It is not so objective as it seems: it is as if we change the map of life itself by changing our attitude towards it. Unfortunately, however, what might be rhythm, harmony and balance between these inner and outer realities, operating reciprocally, becomes upset the instant we defensively project that which belongs within ourselves into the outer world, thereby hoping the better to control it to our immediate advantage. The balance is there still, but now it is the other way, against us in unceasing threatening argument.

At this stage of projection-phantasy, any further insistence upon unity induces the psychology of Paranoia,[1] which, having externalized everything, then experiences emptiness within and feels persecuted by all that external world with which the self was once so hopefully identified. But alas! for the hopes of this poor deluded self. He now feels as if that which he fondly hoped was to be all FOR him is now all AGAINST him, operating as it were at him, by someone's evil purpose. Even the nose which is blown across the road is blown at him, because everything within his own psyche has been projectively attached to everything which belongs to that external reality beyond him.

The fundamental error of every paranoid system is that it must have absolute power, absolute peace and absolute fixed unity. The whole movement of experience is organized in order to provide further evidence of this absolute unity, and it is therefore impermeable to all argument and liable to be extremely aggressive in its self-defence. On the principle that 'this ought to be mine too because all is mine anyway', identification

[1] An intractable form of insanity, characterized by 'projection' and systematized delusions.

has been extended to include everything. Unfortunately, however, there is so much difference between this arbitrarily created self-protective system and the reality in which it lives, that such a mind becomes increasingly detached, isolated and self-opinionated, until finally it becomes socially impossible.

As for persons, so for peoples. The same powers go through the same performances and there is no disorder of the human psyche which cannot be illustrated within the larger world of international relationships. Like dogs and humans, nations also suffer from hysteria. Nations develop paranoia and nations go mad, for the same reasons that individuals undergo these same misfortunes and with the same lack of ultimate advantage. The more we externalize the powers within ourselves, the more the geni is allowed out of the bottle, and the more the snake penetrates, pervasively worming his way into those external domains in which he does not belong, the more we lay ourselves open to persecution by some man-made 'devil'. All this is in spite of the fact that our one hope was for salvation at the benevolent hands of our own particular Saviour.

If these forces had but been developed within ourselves in course of time, they would have become creative, but they become the more destructive as they are more aggressively expiated and externalized. Our private negative forces derived from this inward negative attitude, then become our public persecutors. Whether we know it by that name or not, either as one or many, citizen or state, the label which then applies to our disease is Paranoia, for we have developed the homicidal condition of unteachable insanity.

REALITY

The trouble is that others must suffer for our error. When once we start upon this argument within ourselves, striving to eliminate those 'unpleasant' items which belong within our own psychic structure, the process of internal elimination must also be paralleled upon the undesirable person of an external scapegoat, connection with whom we seek to sever and upon whose neck we wish to strike the timeless separative sword. There must be scapegoats and they must constantly be renewed to satisfy this hungry Moloch, who remains insatiable to the end, for his inward self must always remain unsatisfied. As the aggressive system develops lesser scapegoats are not enough but must become larger still, until the State (through some dictatorial custodian of its 'Honour') can only be satisfied by the declaration of some major war upon an inoffensive neighbour, who has assumed the unwitting rank of persecutor to his system of organized illusion.

Such are the deeper pathways of international mischance. Causes of ill-feeling between nations are so deep in the unseen that it is not to be wondered at that politicians, who are untutored in the mysteries of psychology and practical metaphysics, have not yet developed far in understanding them. Political incidents are the superficially dislodged phenomena of deep psychic movements. Politicians and dictators too, for all their appearance of omnipotent free-will, are but the slaves and puppets of the unseen forces in the national life, which they externally express. They are phenomena of inward meaning, powerless themselves, moved from the unseen, puppets of mass prejudices, externalized. All would-be dictators are possessed rather than possessing, slaves not free, tools in the hands of those unseen forces which are striving for mastery within the deeper life of the unseen.

It has been the particular advantage of the British nation that in its history it has never shown this habit of dependence upon external leadership, and has never believed in seductive offers of salvation or in the verbal messages of Messiahs. Others may like uniforms, drill, words of command and ordered routine, but the collection of individuals who make up our British Commonwealth have always shown a wiser independence, a certain humorous disbelief in quack remedies offered in the political market-place, and a deeper loyalty than that of spectacular leadership. For this reason, if for no other, the British nation now stands alone amidst the flowing tide of mass-movement under dictatorship, a rock in an overwhelming flood of emotional rhetoric, stampeded sanity and angry war cries. But we are also tempted to seek for such leadership. Where is he, where is our saviour? Others have found one, there they go, organized for salvation, so why not us also?

The two opposing tendencies of this our time are on the one hand due to a growth of egotistic nationalism, under the pseudo-mastery of dictators, on the part of nations which are possessed of many of the other manifestations of psychotic disorder; but on the other hand there is evidence of a deeper flowering of the possibilities of individualism, deeply rooted in the unseen, tolerant in time, from whose development there is promise of a renewed harvest of those powers which are hidden within the unseen levels of the self. For the salvation either of the individual or of the nations at

194

this time, we must choose between one and the other. Either we may be led, in a course of aggressive having and doing; or we may be ourselves, independent yet related, free yet disciplined, among, but not identified with, others.

Not outwardly, but inwardly, not externally but deep within the self, is this battle of our time to be fought out to its success or failure. It will be better for us in the end if we can forswear the tempting offers of a Mephistophelian bargain with omnipotence, agreeing instead patiently to internalize all the phenomena of our experience by saying within ourselves: 'Yes I am that,' thus returning our genius to store, our geni to its bottle. From this viewpoint of the tolerant and observant self, we can again regard every manifestation upon the external screen of experience as the image of ourselves to be returned within ourselves, there to join with deeper forces as seeds of darkness, children of the serpent force which is the King of Kings.

Confession and Atonement

At present we are like hounded criminals, in constant and uneasy flight from pursuing justice. Let's get caught, and face the music. Let's see how much of punishment may be required to redress the balance. Like naughty schoolboys, with courage in both hands, let us face the worst, owning up and making full confession.

Unfortunately we have all so gorged ourselves with rights, privileges and possessions to which we are not in fact entitled, that we are loath to ease ourselves even of these somewhat indigestible burdens. It is not only at the dining table that we have overeaten, although this is certainly one of the habits of our time. The process of overeating seems to be universal in our lives, in one way or another. There is so much mental overeating (knowledge), sensorial overeating (entertainment), religious overeating (dogmas, beliefs, prejudices, hopes), commercial overeating (prosperity and wealth). Our needs are dutifully met by an underworld of wage-slaves, who are in general too frightened by insecurity to make it seem worth their while to protest.

We seem to have been taught in terms of possessions, property and security, by our elders and betters who have earlier made the same mistake. We are the products of their philosophy of life and we have been taught it so that it has become not only part of ourselves, but also the most moral part. We feel the 'oughts' so strongly; the 'ought' to possess, the 'ought' to secure, and the 'ought' to fix the security of our possessions. It looks as if, along with much other indigestible material wealth, we have also to give up the very perverse dogma of conventional morality as well.

Meanwhile, battleships become bigger and costlier (because they ought), aeroplanes have become larger and faster (because they ought), business has expanded and knowledge grown (always for the same excellent reason and in the cause of progress). It is not to be wondered at that, with this philosophy of bigger and better busy-bodies, we should now be involved in an acute instability of crisis, which threatens war as imminent and inevitable, not only from one but from many sources. Having gorged, it is difficult to disgorge; and having for so long accepted this false morality, it is difficult to realize the benevolence of that 'death' which is the inevitable wages of our 'sin'. Yet some measure of disgorgement there must be, if we are to find it possible to earn an attitude of peace of mind.

Disgorgement! It does seem a pity to have to pay this penalty for our confession, after our wealth has been collected so carefully, with so much pain and effort, at so much expense, over so long a time. Surely we ought not to sacrifice this empire of the self which the whole world needs as bulwark for security against the rising tide of Bogyism which threatens the very roots of our culture itself? No! Surely our duty is to arm and rearm, thus better to defend the overwhelming privileges of our falling state. Thus cries the endless voice of morality in dire distress, pursuing the endless course of infinite regress.

But it is not enough to defend this egotistic empire, outward or inward, that we have. It is more than likely that we must give it up or have it taken from us, unless there may be still one last chance for us to adopt a less possessive and more realistic, a less fixed and more moving, attitude towards the development of that future history which is being born today. If we have had too much too soon, then we must learn to live on sparer diet, pulling in our belts.

Perhaps we might learn more patience if we could work ourselves instead of employing wage-slaves, growing our food before we cooked it, or cooking it before we ate it. Most people, however, who suffer from indigestion, wish to be allowed to go on eating as much as ever, while being effortlessly, magically, cured. They hope to find some doctor who will allow them even to expand their diet (my dear, he is too marvellous!), so that they can still further enjoy the pleasures of the table, without any restrictions whatsoever. Hopefully, they are again looking for a convenient Messiah, the external saviour who can work the miracle and allow privilege to persist in security. Alas for the better wisdom of these too hopeful ones, there are so many doctors who fall into this trap; as also do parents and teachers, parsons and politicians. They make it impossible to learn until too late.

With so much pain overdue, feeling that there ought to be no pain, sympathy makes it doubly hard for us to accept this need for suffering, either in ourselves or others. We feel that we ought not to be made thus to suffer, and that pain ought not to be inflicted upon others. But this is the same false morality of our times. It is no use trying to escape from suffering or from death. The truth postponed becomes the truth tormenting. There is so much pain in the truth, we need not add to it, but from it we must not subtract. The debit account has been piled up for us and we must pay. The simpler satisfaction of accepted law requires a restoration of balance and a giving way at any price, until relaxation has become an attitude towards life, a philosophy, a religion, and a way of living.

The process of confession, however, which gives up all its beloved defences and securities, does not work to our lasting benefit until and unless it is complete. It must be made utterly without reserve; nothing must be kept back. The ship is not free to sail until the last hawser has been cast loose, the last anchor weighed,

CONFESSION AND ATONEMENT

even the last handclasp let go. It is not enough to give so much and so much; for circulation of the self upon the tide of time, it all must go. Faith is the acceptance of a hopeless and unreasonable task; guilt is the truth, humbly confessed; at-one-ment (which must be peace) is the reward.

CHAPTER V: FORCES FOR WAR

SUMMARY

Dreams.

Hypersensitiveness. The artistic temperament; hyperactivity; organized self-defence; crustacean or vertebrate.

Suggestibility. Defensive identification; suggestibility and war.

Failure of Self-defence. The error of elimination; disaster preferred to suspense; the evil of good intentions.

Resistances. The unclean page of history; the vice of war; vested interests; summary of war-makers.

Speed and Speech. Compulsive action; positive and negative words as bombs or tombs.

Infinite Regress. The vicious circle of our flight from flight; there must be neither force nor magic; the errors of normality.

Neurosis of Normality. The meaning of the 'norm'; set-square and set-fair; the abusive character of 'abnormality'.

Red—Anti-Red. Partisanship; Communism and Fascism; the Bolshevik bogy.

Party Politics. The fallacy of leadership; the emergent

past; propping up and pulling down; discriminative and undiscriminative; politicians and statesmen; democracy and autocracy.

Wealth. Economics; security and gold; the fallacy of
hoarding; the meaning of money.

Money and Work. The morality of labour; earning a
living; making a living; and making money.

Circulation. Unconditional distribution of necessaries.
The Press and advertising; dissipation.

Truth and Insanity. Are we quite mad? What is truth?
Analysis of insanities.

DREAMS[1]

IX. '*The Prize-Winner*'

I was at an Exhibition (like the Brussels or Earls
Court) and I had entered for a competition in which
I had won the prize.

Shirley Temple was there too and she had also won
a prize. I had to go up and get mine with her, and as I
did so I felt that I was holding her high up above the
heads of the crowd.

X. '*Black Magic*'

I was fishing and suddenly I saw an enormous sea
monster emerging from the water. I thought that the
only way I could catch it would be by clapping my
hands together. When I had done so, it jumped out on
the ground by my side and was then only about a foot
long.

[1] For comment, see Appendix (page 306-7).

DREAMS

XI. '*Up and Up*'

I was going up to the top of a very high building of sixty-four stories with my mother. When we got to the top the lift started tipping, and I had that awful feeling of falling. Then we went down two stories and it started tipping again.

My mother appeared very casual and annoyed me by saying: 'Oh, dear, fancy getting stuck here. I wonder if they will be able to send up that beer now.' I was furious that she should fuss about the beer, when it seemed to me to be a matter of life and death.

Chapter V

FORCES FOR WAR

Hypersensitiveness

One of the things that distinguishes a work of art from other works of more mechanical efficiency, is that a work of art is alive; and in this sense the process of our living must be alive to art. Growth implies an inward sensitiveness to circumstances, an ability to make positive adjustment within the self, with due regard to that external movement which is proceeding in the outward world of our experience. Being alive, we are sensitive to our environment; some more than others, for some of us, with more or less of what is called 'artistic temperament', are more sensitive and may rightly be called hypersensitive beyond the average. Although the advantages of such a degree of sensitivity may seem obvious, the disadvantages are liable to be ignored, for there is danger to us all, where feeling may be so easily touched by pain.

If sensitiveness is so much of life, then there is a possibility that those who are most sensitive are also most alive. Unfortunately, however, these are the ones for whom circumstances are most liable to be unduly hard. These 'sensitives' are then induced, both instinctively and by their kindly but shortsighted protectors, to adopt a defensively negative attitude, instead of that positive one which, being the prerogative of life and growth, also belongs to the artists whose task it is thus to manifest it, sensitive, moving and strong. Art is a form of suffering and, whoever else may be excused this penalty of deeper living, artists must suffer. This is one of the laws of life, if its culture is to be true.

As an illustration of attitude to shock, think of the not uncommon domestic misfortune of grasping an electric lamp, the wires of which fuse, giving us a shock. The shock of the sudden impact of electric current upon the sensitiveness of our nervous system first causes muscular tension. We then get rid of it if we can by the actively defensive reaction of hurling it as far away as possible. It is the habit of hypersensitiveness thus to defend itself, contracting inwardly and at the same time acting externally against experience.

But what is wise behaviour with the fused lamp is mere instinctive habit when it comes to the living fireworks of experience. Is it then so wise to defend, contracting both tensely and attentively, in uneasy haste to escape this possibility of pain? The parallel in terms of our digestive processes is to contract and expel, i.e. to vomit; which, though sometimes it may be wise, is not the best technique for us to adopt as general habit, whether our mode of living is that of Art or Science. True, our vomiting may be artistic, for there is an art even of escape, or it may be 'scientific' (let's be reasonable!), but it is nevertheless a manner of rejecting life and not of manifesting it.

This matter of degrees of sensitiveness is most important from the view-point of the teacher, but its study seems to have been neglected. Is this perhaps another example of the way in which we instinctively avoid the possibility of pain? Hypersensitiveness, being a reality of the unseen, seems to have been neglected in a scientific era, which, rightly claiming to be careful in regard to the seen, has nevertheless been notoriously careless and callous in all its dealings with the unseen.

All children are sensitives, some more than others, and therefore not to be treated to severer stimuli than they can positively tolerate. Flowers and fruit are protected from undue frost, so why not children too? But we seem to have dulled ourselves into a state of insensitiveness towards these dumb pleadings of more sentient ones. Children feel the more keenly, although still without consciousness to tell others how or what they feel. They are like other sentient organisms, with power to contract negatively in self-defence, a reaction which may be sometimes seen, but which needs to be felt intuitively if it is to be justly appreciated. There are so many ways of self-defence which adults have acquired. Perhaps this must be so; for instance, if one teacher is to administer educational law to a class of forty little clamouring sentient ones, she needs to be deaf to most if not all of their silent twitterings.

But some may still keep sensitive and live, to become, as artists, teachers of the art of life. For these, if they are to retain their hypersensitiveness living throughout life to the fullest extent, there can only be this one law of learning how to suffer by accepting reality in its full intensity, seen and unseen.

Fully to appreciate the nature of this quality of sensitiveness, it is essential to rid our minds of the encumbering over-simplification induced by the material aspects of the human framework. The psyche is not to be seen merely as head, body, arms and legs, or as this self, now; but as an invisible sensitive organism manifesting through a visible medium, evident in time, but yet expressing a subtler essence of a larger self, a whole of character, from birth to death, eternal. This larger self is related to its circumstance through a material body which has the opportunity of reacting either positively or negatively, accepting experience or defending itself against it. Unfortunately there is always the possibility of 'free-will' (of which more will be said presently), which makes it look to us as if we can change our circumstances, choosing that which we shall accept and rejecting that which we prefer to eliminate.

It is easier by far, however, to change ourselves defensively, by adopting a negative attitude. When once this process of negative defensiveness has become a habit, to that extent our attitude towards life becomes negative and growth becomes distorted. These NO's have become KNOTS, kinks in the character of subsequent development. Life can never be the same again, until we have learnt to accept in full that which we have once rejected in our past experience. Although we may be living 'now' in all appearances, we are yet actually manifesting our past refusals to live, and all of us are to some extent thus handicapped by past experience. We are not living now, but THEN; we are like unruly children, undisciplined to fact in spite of our grey hairs. We either live nervously and negatively, or falsely in some defensive illusion of our own creation, which we urgently insist is real, forcing it too upon others not so well protected. We must, because we need to do so. We use our defensive systems like spectacles for weak eyes, or crutches for a limb long paralysed.

There are many such illusions, which were listed in a previous chapter under the general title of 'Forms of Aggressiveness', including both rationalism and 'religion', efficiency and work, humour and a masculine attitude towards life. In this way we create an assumed reality which becomes fixed in a condition which we regard as 'normal', but which may in fact well be a state of individual or social neurosis.

Whether this organization of a defensive system is that of the individual psyche or of society in general, it is largely a false pattern or shell worn with an ulterior motive. Although unconsciously devised for gain, the once vertebrate self has now become a crustacean, and what it has gained by its defensive adaptability, it has lost in creative freedom. This protective habit presents us with an apparent reality, as real as any other to the sensitive. Living within this shell of circumscription, or within that larger shell of social circumstance, we may regard ourselves as 'normal'. But if there is evidence of uneasy movement, our instability makes us liable to be placed in the category of 'neurotics'. If it breaks altogether, we may well feel afraid that we are 'insane'. Society does not encourage hypersensitives by more generous labels.

For our encouragement in such adversity, however, we may realize that this shell of so-called 'normality' or social custom is only a neurotic defence mechanism, by

o   209

some most effectively assumed. Within this false façade, it is the hypersensitive (he is the best not worst, for his encouragement) who will prove most uncomfortable, and who will most easily fall into the classification of the neurotics. What might have counted as advantage becomes doubly disadvantage when it is defensively measured against the generally accepted standards of a false attitude towards life. Values are relative, and, afraid of so much isolation, we do not sufficiently trust our own.

Suggestibility

The problem of hypersensitiveness leads naturally to a consideration of the meaning of suggestibility, which deserves special consideration in connection with any discussion of the motives concerned in Peace and War. Like many other words, it is frequently used without sufficient consideration of its meaning. In what is it wrong, and what virtues does this attitude contain, if any?

It has already been suggested that the harm does not reside in hypersensitiveness, but in protective hyperactivity. The virtue of suggestibility is that it is a faculty of sensitiveness, or acuteness of perception; the suggestible person is open to receive, and does. But what then? Its harm is that sensitiveness is then used defensively, as a protective identification occurs with the object, whatever it may be. This is not merely laziness; it is also intensely purposive in a defensive way. It avoids the intolerable suspense of thought: but more than that, it offers a form of action that also solves the problem by assuming its successful conclusion.

SUGGESTIBILITY

The error of suggestibility is therefore in the fact that we identify ourselves with objects or opinions, especially if these are invested with power, such as words (which are symbols) or conventions (which are safeguards against too great a feeling of difference). The common error is mass suggestibility, in which the sense of universal brotherhood is perverted to a mere practice of imitating others in self-defence. This is the fallacy of all neurotic minds, who always make defensive adjustments in order to avoid the pressing problem of their doubts.

In war suggestibility comes into its own, for action is then at a premium. With one accord, in self-defence, we obey the dictatorship of this unseen command, and moralize it, the better to feel sure this 'ought' to be.

In all suggestibility there can be no true relationship, because of the false unification which has thus been defensively fixed. Relationship demands duality and difference. But the way of peace demands above all that this difference, and its accompanying suspense, should prove acceptable. The problem must then be seen where it belongs; namely, between subject and object, in the attitude towards life. Can we think and live, not only for ourselves, but also amongst others?

The way of the hypersensitive is hard because there are so many differences to register, so much friction and ill-usage to contend with, so much helpful advice offered, and so many orders given that seem to clamour for obedience. It is hard to feel the truth, but easy to accept opinions as to what is best: it is hard to hold the balance tolerantly in suspense, but easy to act in urgent morality identified with a 'good' cause.

But there can be no peace for those who are suggestible, since voices differ and opinions change. The simpler way is to be more truthful, and honesty is the best policy for peace. But it requires the courage to stand alone amidst life's battles, sensitive but not necessarily active, poised in spite of pushing to the contrary, different but related, as an integrated and sincere Self.

The Failure of Defensiveness

Unfortunately this defensive habit, the purpose of which was to effect some gain, owing to the way in which it strives to escape from the unseen, finds itself finally on the wrong side of paradox, losing instead. The negative or defensive attitude will always be liable to ally itself with the enemy from whom it is so anxious to escape, owing to this instinctive urge which presents itself under the guise of good. A simple example of such a defence mechanism is that of the nervous wife who anxiously awaits her husband's return. He said he would be back by seven o'clock and by seven-thirty she has made up her mind that he has suffered some terrible accident and that she will never see him again. A few minutes later he arrives cheerfully and in good health, armed with some reasonable excuse, and is surprised to be greeted by an aggressive woman who now seems only anxious to eliminate him. This is because she has the eliminative attitude towards suspense, which she cannot tolerate, and the worst kind of certainty was preferable to the agony of doubt. The same eliminative process is transferred to greet him on his return, because she has this instinctive habit of

212

thus defending herself against every unseen aggressor.

This same neurotic defensive process is clearly manifested in the relationships between one nation and another. If there is any doubt as to what is happening across the national border, there is a strong tendency towards the adoption of an aggressive attitude in self-defence, not so much against the enemy personally as against the state of intolerable suspense. War is provoked by our own attitude of intolerance towards the danger of it. We are inclined to precipitate a disaster rather than face the nature of it. It is not enough to pile up defensive armaments: the growth of intolerable strain will lead to war illogically devised in order to avoid an unknown danger. The fear of uncertainty suggests the obviously fallacious conclusion that the gap of our suspense is better filled, even with disaster. Anything seems preferable to suspense.

There is always this centrifugal force urging us to do something defensively about the unseen problem. There is an urge to move from A to B, unseen to seen, female to male, feeling to knowledge, until we have eventually become positively identified with the enemy himself, and self with circumstance. This process leads in the end to a state of infinite regress. In flight from our own inward selves, the enemy becomes projected until we have become our own enemies, fighting that other one outside ourselves who really all the time belongs inside. The negative attitude, once it has become established with its moral urge of betterment, leads increasingly to its own defeat. The more we strive to improve the situation, the worst it becomes.

It is for this reason that all disorder in the vital pro-

cesses of the mind is so difficult for the self to heal. The
error is one of initial judgment, and the yardstick by
which we measure our experience is itself fallacious.
Every time we use it we come to the same wrong
conclusion, and the more we apply our eliminative
methods to get rid of the offender, the more entram-
melled we become in our attachment to him. Europe
in hysterical panic is not going to be cured by the
hysterical efforts of intolerant leadership, or by those
who would find escape by crying 'Peace'. There can
be no cure of this disease apart from a full digestion
or acceptance of the unpalatable meal of facts, both
past and present, however often their unsavoury details may have been refused. The negative attitude
must be changed to positive, before the flight of an infinite regress can be set free from the vicious circle of
its own momentum.

Our minds thus moving upon the surface of experience are liable to get judgment inverted, because we are
unable to see the other part of paradox which is always
included in the whole of reality. It seems so simple to
us, placed at a point in space and time and not realizing
the movement of life, to hold things fixed and good.
Our purposes seem adequate, and we are unaware of
the ulterior motives which are the real determinent of
so many of our actions. There is so much confusion between inward and outward reality, between self and
state, between my advantage and yours with whom I
am identified, that it seems as if it must be inevitable
that all our efforts towards peace can only effect the
opposite result. Every direct effort, every ulterior motive, every aggressive attempt to eliminate the unde-

sirable, adds more fuel to the threatening flames of war.

Yet our trouble is not with evil purpose, but with good, misunderstood and misapplied. We mean so well, but since we are standing on our heads, our best intentions seem to come out on the wrong side of paradox. Our energy so forcefully applied defeats its own peaceful end. We hoped to fix this peace and feel surprised that so we have made war more threatening: for to try to fix movement is vice indeed, to pinch us the more painfully.

Science and mechanics engineer our slaughter, but there are other salesmen who induce us to buy these dubious advantages. Who are they? What forces push us in the path of war, and who are they who insistently clamour that we should follow their blind leadership?

Resistances

Of itself, the way of peace is not an easy way, because its own simplicity is hard enough in practice. Working against it, however, there are many resistances which must first be recognized before they can be overcome. It always seems so much easier to appeal to the need for instant change, to turn over a new leaf, as if the past can be rewritten by the simple process of turning over a page. Such swift conversion, however, is only another disguise for the eliminative factor of aggressive self-defence. It is one of the fallacies based upon 'I must-have-now'. The page upon which we are to write is not and never can be clean. The past, whether it refers to the individual or to the history of Europe and its related nations, is not thus to be dealt with by a stroke of the pen, the fixing of a boundary or the signing of a peace treaty, however high the hope or pious the intention. Such methods are disease, not cure. The very idea itself of instant change for good resembles a magical gesture, which claims its own omnipotence under the dictatorship of undisciplined desire. The dubious gift of our free-will is not thus to be manifested, but rather by the disciplined acceptance of reality as it is, moving and growing in space and time, which includes the fullest recognition of the effect which the past must always have in determining our present situation. The cause of today is not to be found today in the seen, but yesterday in the unseen; for today's history was written yesterday and tomorrow's is being written today, although not in just the way that we would choose.

The resistances which today obstruct a better way of peace are numerous, and they are not by any means only due to obviously neurotic factors or to the urgency of unrighteous egotism. Peace must be alive: it is movement in suspense, a fact of living growth. But it always seems as if freedom to grow introduces too much danger, as if the worst might happen unless we force ourselves to interfere, by fixing some advantage to encourage doubt. If we regard this intolerance of suspense (which is a necessity for living movement in time) as the first evidence of neurotic instability, then the whole force of it is marshalled upon the side of war and against a more peaceful procedure. There has been so much of past injustice and aggressive interference, that solution of the present problem is made thereby more difficult. But the present problems are not thus to be solved by repeating the anxious methods which have bred them in the past.

What are the forces against peace, and in whose hands? Who operates this vice of war and why? It would be so much easier if we could be sure that our enemies were obvious, but it is not so. We have to recognize the aggressive influence in so many places, exercised in so many ways: especially, however, in the ulterior motives of those politicians who are inclined to solve their own problems vicariously in national disguise, leading to a degree of earnestness which provokes further misunderstanding. There are vested interests, developed and sanctified as normal structures in the organization of the Church and State, which have become fixtures that would arouse bitterest resentment at any suggestion that they should be moved.

In ourselves we prefer seen to unseen, fixed to moving, known to unknown. We all have to some extent this intolerance of the unseen and this determination to justify our own development in the way that seems best to us, in order to establish our footing in circumstances which seem to be (to say the least of it) unfriendly. Where so much operates against peace, it is not to be wondered at that we should find ourselves moving rapidly in the direction of war. Individual and social politics are organized that way, and unless we can individually and socially develop a different organization we shall fail to solve these problems of international crisis with which we are presented at this time.

We may summarize the list of forces acting on the side of war as follows:

(a) The tendency towards differentiation and resistance against change. This is a function of the
thought process itself, which measures difference and
makes comparison, such as: 'This is not that, this is
better than that.' The moral judgment follows, usually
without doubt: 'This ought to be that'. We want to be
ourselves, and resent interference.

(b) Information derived from senses is also derived
from recognition of difference. It tells us of pleasure or
of pain, and instinct will choose the one and reject the
other. To live according to the dictatorship of reason,
consciousness, senses, or conscience, any or all, will lead
us towards war.

(c) Desire itself must be inclined towards aggressiveness, even the desire for peace. Desire is not to be
trusted, because it is always personal. The universal life
transcends desire, but life within any personal limits
requires war to protect its frontiers.

(d) Desire is usually complicated, however, by ulterior motives, so that we seem to want not for ourselves but for others. The mother 'unselfishly' wants
the advantage of her children, but is this unselfish if
she has identified herself with them? The teacher
anxiously promotes the progress of his class, but is this
good for anyone if he is 'sublimating' his own un-
realized ambitions? The politician is sure the other
side is wrong, but what of the projection of his own
repressed unrest? The statesman is solely interested in
his country's welfare, but what if his country has become confused with his own insatiable egotism? . . . If
desire is dangerous for peace, then ulterior motives are
always fatal to it.

(e) Defence against the uncertainty of suspense fixes advantage and privilege wherever possible by treaty or promise, customs barrier or 'favoured nation' clause. Anxiety covers up the unseen, which is doubtful, by the seen, which is 'set fair'. Then credit owes its debit, and misfortune waits upon tomorrow's innocents who are called upon to pay. If they should persist in trying to hold up a falling structure, the debt to be paid eventually by unseen posterity becomes exceedingly great.

(f) Vested interests are innumerable and no one who is enjoying them can bear to think they should be sacrificed for any larger cause. They become moralized: 'This is so, and so this ought to be; it must continue!' The organizations of vested interests are terrifically powerful, including banks and commerce, law and schools, and the various churches and political bodies. They must support themselves, or feel the world itself is coming to an end. They cannot see the force of paradox, or that they need to change because their world is coming to an end.

(g) Habit is strong: what was, is, and the past is present with us, living now. We are fettered to the past, and these fetters are strong and subtly forged. Only growth from deeper roots will change our habits, but they cannot be knocked off by wilful interference. Education is the best hope here, but bad habits meanwhile need not be offered the privileges of leadership.

(h) *Relativity*. This is a metaphysical point, but as such it is very important. To change one is to change all. If father says 'turn' and does, then we needs must all turn too, if only a little, to make more room for him.

Society is too closely organized to permit of anyone changing without some influence being felt all round. Part of the law of life says 'All is movement'; another part reads 'For any movement, some resistance must be overcome'. Our world is Relative, but unfortunately we think it Absolute, and any such false fixing must be aggressively sustained.

Speed and Speech

Now we are off, and speech vies with speed to tell the world about it.

If action is compulsive and we feel that we must do something to ease the strain of our unrest, in speed and speech we have most admirable means, for both are worthy of much praise today. Although less talked about than speed, speech has also surpassed all records of recent years, and each year adds more words upon the air. For fight as well as flight, we have both speed and speech to serve us.

Like all else, speed and speech may be used either positively or negatively, i.e. to go somewhere or say something, or to escape. If they were more positively used, there would be more silence and more rest. There is not so much to say: and as for going somewhere else, the most important place is where we are. Distance is a surface phenomenon, which is reduced to nothing at the centre, from which however we are so anxious to depart. We always moralize our crime: and so we must feel sure that so much speed is good. We say that it brings us so much nearer to our neighbours, and thus makes friendship easier than it was before. But somehow it does not seem to work that way, and these records are more competitive than co-operative in their results.

In terms of centre and circumference, the further we are from the centre the faster we must move, for speed and time (duration) both depend upon the length of this our radius. Therefore to find peace and sleep, we must move again towards this centre, falling centripetally. The opposite extreme of centrifugal flight requires sustained effort, as rising upon aggressive wing we climb and climb until perhaps we burst, and so create another record. The further we go, the greater the speed and the greater our sense of worthy competition. Flying thus, we must go on and on in flight: it seems too hard to stop and too disturbing to our balance. So flight and speed become our virtue, and we feel convinced that we ought to go still faster.

But it is most doubtful whether these days of speed will be viewed by subsequent history as any more worthy of praise because of the speed with which we met disaster. We may have behaved according to the habit of bursting bombs, with no respect for time except as some enemy to be eliminated or vacuum to be filled, but Speed is no virtue. It is a symptom of the self's unrest, and measures lack of balance. We are not to be praised for it: it must be so, because it is part of present pattern, and is one other compulsion forced upon us by our cowardice and greed.

And so is speech, for again we cannot stop. Where silent spaces seem so bad a thing, there must be many praises for the broadcast word to cover everything. These spaces must be filled, and so they are—dutifully, instructively, amusingly and carefully, word by word, each space is filled with speech. We feel that something has been wasted if time is not thus filled; or that evil might perhaps enter into a space that was not papered from floor to ceiling with information and instructions.

When anxiously we look upon the consequences of our foolishness and see the danger of impending disaster, we feel sure that something must be done in self-defence. Our enemy looks threatening, and so we turn to speech, because of all uneasy action, talking is cheapest flight from fact, and easiest moralized. 'I think we ought to say something to him about it!' carries portentous weight, and unfortunately seems most formidable, words being the weapons which they are. However, it is not words or truth that count, but the motive beneath, or spirit of the matter. If that is positive (love, courage), no harm will come even from attempting to put truth in words. If it is negative, however (hate, flight), the verbal truth is as aggressive as any other way of timeless flight from fact.

Poor League of Nations! What a magnificent façade was that for fools to hide behind. It was not crime that they discussed, but the very platitudes of virtue. A spate of words builds a fine tomb for Peace; indeed, there is no better way of burying it than by a Peace Conference, which is so very virtuous in so many words.

It is strange how much we have forgotten of the ways of children, who use words endlessly, meaninglessly, bluffingly, experimentally, protectively, magically. We call them 'chatterbox' and know that it is idle make-believe. But when it comes to grown-up men in Parliaments and Conferences and Committees, we fail to see that the same young tricks are being played again.

Written or spoken word, they are like spots upon our skin; they are more various and ruddy, but they are symptoms of the disease within. Speech and speed: speed and speech; between these two we live (or is it that we flee from life?). They are part of the pattern that must be fulfilled until the debt is paid, the sickness cured and victim healed. Thus are all symptoms linked, so that not one of them can be healed apart from all the others, without some other symptom coming swiftly in to take its place. Both doctors and statesmen need whole views, for life and men and circumstance are one.

The Infinite Regress

In whatever way we may choose to build our social structure, it will tend to organize itself accordingly. It is the outward and visible sign of what we are, and how we feel about life. It is more than we deserve; it is as we have made it, because of what we are. As society is aggressive, so we must have been aggressive to make it so; if we are negative, so is the society in which we live; if we fix, so does society; if we would run away from deeper reality, so does society make it easy for us to do so, organizing for us a multitude of easy methods of escape. We are society.

The dead hand of flight has touched so much that might have been of more creative worth. The negative attitude predominates, being negative even to itself, in infinite regress; flight, flight from flight, flight from flight from flight . . . in a vicious circle, *ad infinitum*. The wheel of life goes widdershins, which is black magic, when it might have been so white. But magic itself seems to us today to be evil, being born of the unseen. Today we must despise the dark ages for their belief in witchcraft, and Africa for its belief in the efficacy of magic. If witchcraft may yet be true, and if there be some truth in magic, then where does the progress of our vaunted reason stand?

But so the order has gone forth. There must be no magic nowadays. Even the churches make no claim to it, preferring the colder rights of reason. Science knows nothing of forces, but only of the things which those unseen forces move. Political systems work by rule of thumb, ordering people how they are to live. Doctors prescribe, but, knowing little of the reason why, they can have little faith in anything but heroic surgery, and in the patient's quite unreasonable ability to recover. They have never been taught how to make people healthy (i.e. positive), but only how to eliminate disease (i.e. negative about negative).

Having so fled from force, we have externalized it and thus lost the control which we might have over our destiny. And now, beset by dictators, seen and unseen, we are still inclined to say: 'There must be no force! We must not use force, for it is a bad thing.' We can only see peace in terms of flight, even from death. Then who will hold for us this firework which is life?

Science carefully measures the seen, but it despises the unseen. Religion subdivides itself, protesting and nonconforming in one negative schism after another, pursuing the path of infinite regress while aggressively attaching itself to the altars of efficient organization. Art exploits a multiplication of accurate imitations; its greatest novelty is 'Surrealism', which prides itself upon its ability to escape all the limitations imposed upon

224

sanity by reality. Education is more or less free for all, but the originality of individualism suffers mechanization by mass-production methods, and top marks are awarded for aggressive excellence. The limits of law aggressively insist that the aggressive should be aggressively eliminated, thus establishing the right by means of out-wronging the wrongdoer. Our amusements are catered for by mechanized methods, for we cannot amuse ourselves. Those who cannot play football themselves, enthusiastically shout and boo the gallant but well-paid efforts of others in ardent partisanship. Those who can neither run nor take a risk, back horses. Those who cannot take the trouble to tolerate silence have sound brought to their ears without effort, or go to picture palaces to enjoy the vicarious advantages of a synthetic cinema version of the culture of our age.

This system we call normality, and it is to live in this disordered world that we bring up our children so expensively. The system is threatened with disaster, but we have no thought but to hold it up, while we clamour for peace in which to enjoy it. Because we live in it, it seems to be as sacred as ourselves. This way of living as refugees from realism, this vaunted palace of progress and culture, it must never suffer change. It is normal to be so! Who said so? And what does this word normal mean?

The Neurosis of Normality

That which is average and usual may too easily escape our criticism. Perhaps we need another footrule and set-square, with which to measure a moving universe in such moving times as these, than that which seemed true enough for measuring out the limits of a lesser-dimensional world. If peace is to be experienced as living, then is any other standard than a four dimensional one likely to be enough? Three-dimensional norms we know, they are sufficient for reasonable measurement. But are they enough to live by? Is it enough to be set-square normal? Or is there another norm of four-dimensional worth, living, moving and relative?

Of course, if we are seeking for the best means of escape from the movement of reality, there is no doubt whatever that the best means of all is to be what convention considers to be 'normal'. Normality is the paradise of escapeologists, for it is a fixation concept, pure and simple. It is something which, being normal, is therefore beyond criticism. It is itself a standard, and therefore not to be touched, as is shown by the aggressive use of such abusive epithets as 'abnormal' or 'unusual', 'neurotic' or 'insane'.

But movement never came from such normality; in fact, it must always come in spite of it. 'The boy is not normal!' Then perhaps there is a chance he may be something better, more alive, himself, unique. If he is to be so great a pioneer, however, then there is a penalty of difference that must be born without aggressiveness before it can become effective. Society makes it difficult to feel different without some sense of being outcast, criminal, impossibly alone. It offers the way of escape by infinite regress, aggressively, eliminatively. It is far easier for us all to fall to the temptation of being 'normal', complying with the pattern of a false prophet of some defensive system. But it is bet-

ter, if we can, to stand alone and to feel quite normal
about our abnormality, doing nothing whatever about
it, except what needs to be done in order to be oneself.

The sense of difference is beset by a benevolent
morality, however, to bend it back again. 'You ought
to be like us, you ought not to be different.' The crowd
is always afraid of lonely ones, who will not obey the
dictatorship of herd morality. They must be educated
back to the fold, and in fact, mechanically, they usually
are. The weight of the herd is very strong. Intolerance
on the defensive, urges its rights upon us until it is
difficult to be other than Oxford or Cambridge, Red
or Blue, Right or Left, this church or that. There is
such safety in these labels and in the fixed assurance
that the other side is wrong.

Red—Anti-Red

Partisanship is the outward effort to restore lost inward balance. We are all possessed to some extent of
this inward dis-ease, that seems to cry for rescue by
attachment to the leader of some virtuous cause.
Oxford or Cambridge, East or West, Red or Blue, the
inward image must split again upon the surface of the
outward mirror, clamouring that this side should win,
but that the other should be thrown down.

It is particularly in politics that we are thus the
victims of our own unrest. Today we see the opposing
armies of Red and Anti-Red, which represent respectively the Left and Right banks of the river of Life. The
Bolshevik Bogy is the everlasting Dragon: his heroic
enemy is our friend St. George, impetuous as ever in

his desire to interfere. These two are met and measured, balanced antagonists, such that the growth of one is equalled by the opposite efforts of the other. As one growls, so must the other roar; as in a mirror, the threatening fist of one induces an equal and opposite gesture of revenge. Red promotes the swelling wrath of Anti-Red, and Anti-Red's anger causes Red to grow, as the vicious circle draws its life from aggressiveness about aggressiveness.

The growth of Communism is an evidence of the increasing power of collectivism, the unseen reality of common sense in universal man. But if this four-dimensional reality is used three-dimensionally, it is no better than our best friend turned worst enemy. Fascism also represents the power that belongs to groups, but it again is misapplied to personal advantage. Both Red and Anti-Red contain this fact in common, that they claim to speak for all, yet apply their power for one against the rest. Collectivism, Communism, groups of all kinds, must learn the larger sense of the universal truth, which is unconditional in the brotherhood of man, of excluding none and loving all, before their practice can reach the level of their preaching. But this method is not in them yet.

Meanwhile, we must learn that inverted evil cannot make good. Aggressiveness itself is wrong, breeding aggressiveness with added strength to the opposing side. The way of peace in politics, as ever, is to act as mediator to these opposing forces which are ranged against one another. This is not to say that we are sentimentally to deny difference around a conference table, creating a fog or formulæ to cover our distress, behind which the forces of evil are more free to bring disaster. On the other hand, our method must be to define and accept all differences that may be true in fact. There is more discipline required to watch with endless accuracy, than to talk peace at conferences, or to act virtuously by way of noble example. The referee in this match must not take sides, but must even be prepared to judge himself, if his capacity as illuminator is to bring peace into the warring ways of less far-seeing men.

Party Politics

Aristotle's statement that some men by nature are made worthy to command, others only to serve, may be true enough, but it forms a dubious foundation for our citizenship. Leaders and led is false dichotomy where all must serve the state, if the state is to be well served.

There is so much fallacy in this matter of leadership, that we must pursue these chosen ones with questions: What are you doing in front, and why? You are so very earnest with yourselves in others' welfare, why so disinterested? What took you into politics, and who chose you thus to be leaders of men?

The first answer to suggest is also the rudest. It is well known that those who are unable to mind their own business must always have a finger in someone else's pie. A mind which cannot balance itself seeks external support to lean on, and then feels sure that its activities must be the more disinterested, seeing that they are about someone or something else. When young, children like to play at being engine drivers;

229

when grown in years, though not necessarily in wisdom, they may devote themselves to the more serious task of politics for the same reason. Lacking so much of self that matters, we seek for power, by obtaining a portion of privilege in regard to others.

The adopted policy of our political colour must be pursued the more urgently, because of the unseen depth of its unconscious drive. The emergent past makes itself felt in present pattern, where nursery problems enforce certain attachments to authority or rebellions from it, according to earlier experience. Party principles, so sure of right and wrong, are but a complex of ulterior motives externally projected the better to safeguard the unseen self. In dead earnest, if we are successful in our appeal to the public, we are now qualified for leadership, and may become part of an organization possessed of one of the finest club houses in the world: the House of Commons.

The problems that present themselves to our roving missionary with a political eye are very numerous, but may first be over-simplified by classifying them into 'Propping up' and 'Pulling down', plus or minus, Yes or No, to *status quo*. 'This must stay, but that must go.' (See Diagram 20, page 231.) We see him thus engaged upon his lifelong task of holding up a falling structure with one hand whilst pulling down a rising threatening one with the other; until such time as a turn in the electoral tide shall put an end to his dubious opportunity for service to the state.

The alternative to such a divided policy of escape is Statesmanship, which not only transcends the clash of party strife, but also rises above national differences.

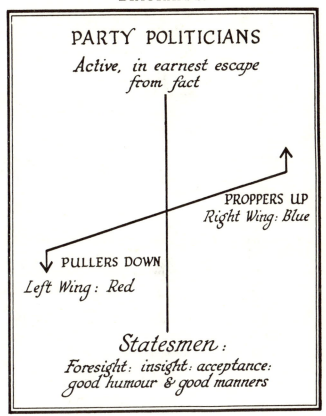

DIAGRAM 20

PARTY POLITICIANS

Active, in earnest escape from fact

PROPPERS UP
Right Wing: Blue

PULLERS DOWN
Left Wing: Red

Statesmen :
Foresight: insight: acceptance: good humour & good manners

This requires a man, however, who has transcended the problems of his own oppressive nature, and has learnt the effective discipline of minding his own business. But why then should he bother with the unruly game of politics, having a full mastery of his own kingdom? He does not need to lead, for he is himself a leader. However, he may be born to rule, entering politics as a natural walk in life. Then we may find true statesmanship; but how much opportunity will he find to rise amongst others, whose earnestness is so much more clamorous than his own?

The instinctive classification of political parties is bilateral, and it is no better than instinctive in the method of government which it employs. It is fundamentally and blindly, unconsciously and defensively, discriminative according to the simplest possible classification: Right and Wrong, Right and Left, Blue and Red, Up with This and Down with That. Being based on instinct, it is emotional, lacking both insight and foresight. Being unconscious, it is blind to reality, and being defensive it is aggressive in its inclination to defeat every movement which seems to suggest the existence of the unseen hand of some evil enemy. (See Diagram 21, page 233.)

There is another alternative, however, which is the Undiscriminating attitude in politics. This maintains that all men are brothers and so there must be no offensive argument amongst them. This classification we must also subdivide into 'Sitters on the fence' and 'Accepting Realists'. The former maintain the uneasy balance of their perch by saying 'No' to both sides, thus living by a double negative. The latter, however, are sustained by the double acceptance of both sides, as indeed of all matters that are 'true'. These are political realists, statesmen again; the silent few, true Radicals. Their opposite numbers are idealists, pacifists, religious devotees, sincerely sentimental; so near and yet

DIAGRAM 21

POLITICS

1. *Discriminative*

(a) LEFT *(Red)*

Youth v. Old Age

(b) RIGHT *(Blue)*

Old Age v. Youth

2. *Undiscriminative*

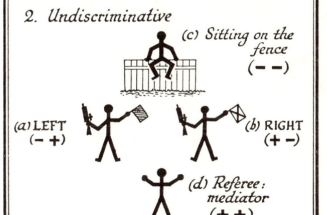

(c) Sitting on the fence
(- -)

(a) LEFT
(- +)

(b) RIGHT
(+ -)

(d) Referee:
mediator
(+ +)

so far from the truth, separated from it by that narrow hair's breadth that makes them dearest enemies.

In all men there is some light, but it looks as if politicians are so blindly led by their own unconscious impulses that they are peculiarly qualified to lead the blind into the ditch. There is in Democracy, however, a subtle sensitiveness to this danger which protects us somewhat against the evil of a too effective government. Unconscious processes always have a way of cancelling one another out, and this is true for our democracy.

The electorate votes; not all of it, but most people like to exercise occasionally this freedom to make the gesture, thus demonstrating the integrity of their own free-will. The successful candidate is proclaimed amidst tremendous enthusiasm (instinctive emotional partisanship is always thus). But thousands are now entirely voiceless in the government, and other thousands are represented only by this one, who must himself speak with his party's voice on all matters of importance. Successful candidates divide the elected house into this side and that, which is an admirable arrangement for the display of debate, while matters are arranged behind the scenes. Everyone is sufficiently dissatisfied by this nullification of the spirit of adventure to express disapproval. But since, as at Hyde Park Corner, we are still free to talk, honour and free-will are duly satisfied and all is well. Movement is at a minimum, the *status quo* is safely statuesque, and democratic government has proved its wisdom by reducing leadership to an impotent farce, a pleasant show, a gratifying performance, in fact to anything but an opportunity for action. All is well, and the life of the people is thus maintained through the perils of protective paradox.

Democracy is magnificently inefficient. Thus it excels, until a totalitarian and autocratic rule crops up somewhere else, to threaten its genius for inefficiency with disaster.

Obviously, autocracies and dictatorships must always be more efficient than democracies, for the simple reason that they not only can do things, but actually get them done. They can change a people in a generation, for better or worse. But to change one nation is to force change also upon its neighbours; change one, and all must change. Then the uneasy instinct of democracy feels threatened from the unseen, and, missing the true genius for ineffective leadership, seeks for leaders so that something may be done. The cry is 'Leaders for defence'; and search is made for scapegoats that sacrifice may be offered to the gods once more, and thereby the projected contents of the vials of wrath may be appeased. The instinct of escape orders an efficiency of armament and the life's blood of the community is shed financially in thousands of millions of pounds, which surely might be better spent than upon the engines of destruction. Escape, escape, the only thought; but a vicious circle offers little hope for the future, however efficient our leaders may be in adding to its destructive impulse.

For the effective government of a country, very little requires to be done; in fact the less that is done the better. The trouble about all dictatorships is that they are invested with so much power that they are able to get things done which in most cases would be better left undone, or at least done in more timely fashion, while more is seen of underlying fact. The urge to be up and doing requires just the cancellation which it so effectively receives under democratic government, but all is in danger of unlimited licence when government is in the hands of some dictatorship, however benevolent may be its first intentions. Leaders are best in the service of their country when they are least able to produce a sudden change. The movement of any living culture should be determined by its own growth, not by the anxious egotism of urgent and self-willed dictatorship. We need more vision, less action; but efficient leadership, anxious to escape, is all for seeing nothing, but getting something done.

The peculiar genius of the British race has always been that it has not lived by leadership. Some inward sense of fun assails us when we see important people; their splendid uniforms fail to hide the ridiculous, and pompous promises arouse suspicion that the man is not to be trusted at his own valuation. There is something deep in the heart of our collective being which seems silently to repeat: 'The kingdom is within you; don't be misled by offered leadership to some more distant political paradise.'

There is some danger now that seeking better we may find still worse. Faced by crisis, we may seek salvation by leadership as other nations have done. But there is something better for our race than that, some better service for our time. It is that we may show our native genius for reality even in politics, and thus prove to others in our changing times the fallacy of promises, and the deeper need for discipline in the face of painful fact. Although it may seem easier to be led out than to go through, we must go through these perilous times, first each within ourselves, alone, and then together.

Wealth

Apart from political differences, the most important external fact operative in regard to peace and war is the system of Economics which exists within and between different nations. In regard to this, it is very plain that the psychological factor of anxiety is of fundamental importance. The order of events is in the hands of blind defensive instinct firmly entrenched behind the protective mask of reason, and the 'Must-Haves' are trying to have it all their own way. Economic systems which are based upon the assumption of fixation of security or value are neurotic both in principle and in practice, because the wealth of a country is like its health—it is alive, and therefore based on four-dimensional laws of movement, in spite of all instinctive error to the contrary. The attempt to fix wealth by an economic system, or peace by treaties, is bound to fail, because both wealth and peace (if they are to be alive) belong not in the fixed three-dimensional system but in the moving four-dimensional one. Fixation is a type of misapprehension in the body politic, that is allied to constipation in the physical system.

It is strong evidence in favour of the fallacy of leadership that so many apparently first-class minds have failed to realize the nature of our economic problems. They cannot advise us with uncertain voice, but hesitate between gold standard or no gold standard, spend-

DIAGRAM 22

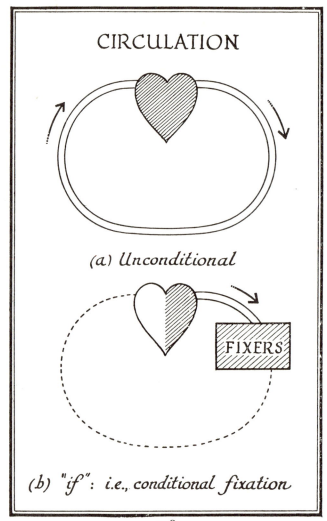

CIRCULATION

(a) Unconditional

(b) "if": i.e., conditional fixation

ing or saving, arguing in favour of this or that policy from time to time. There is no certainty anywhere, even on behalf of orthodoxy, as to which should be the right policy for us to adopt. Meanwhile some countries hoard gold, regarding it as a symbol of security; or they hoard wealth with a view to establishing themselves in an impregnable position; or they build up armaments, hoping that bigger guns and better battleships will be able to fix their security for them. But the hope of fixing any such security in a moving world is fallacious, and the God of Gold is a false god, who can do nothing but harm in the long run to his worshippers.

The trouble, however, is not so much with gold or any single thing in itself, as it is with the fallacy of hoarding, which is determined by our attitude towards the thing we value. Who are these fixers who feel so sure that it is their bounden duty to lay on one side the lifeblood of the community, in order to keep it there for the community's welfare? They are the leaders of finance and industry, but they are all three-dimensional fixers, they are neurotic in method and aggressive to a dangerous degree. In the process of this instinctive idolatry of external values, money has received an extreme degree of pseudo-religious moralization, so that its value has been changed from that of a ticket in lieu of a commodity, until it has itself become the most important commodity of all. Instead of being a means to an end for the circulation of goods, it has become an end in itself, for the merit of its own hoarding.

In Diagram 22, page 238, the role of the economists and bankers is illustrated as operating upon a circulating process by the majesty of their benevolent inter-

ference, laying up gold and stores of wealth which may
be allowed occasionally to circulate in a limited way,
conditional upon various rules of applied usury. However small the percentage of interest charged may be,
it has to be very clearly understood that every principle
of applied usury is fallacious, and that every process of
hoarding acts effectively as a withdrawal from the vital
circulation. These fixers are labouring under the misapprehension that, in the long run of life, anybody is
going to benefit thereby; but it has become such a part
of the system, that any suggestion of interference with
our financial control is regarded as a very dangerous
and subversive heresy. It is worse nowadays than an
attack upon God, because money is in effect the only
god that matters.

But money is in fact only a ticket, a permission to
move goods, a means and not an end. Its purpose is to
facilitate circulation, and yet in our neurotic system
it has become the surest method of impeding it. We
live today in an era of property fixation, the law of
which is effectively organized by the must-haves for the
illusion of their best security. The seen is worth more
than the unseen, and thus the motor car as a symbol of
property is more sanctified by our legal processes than
the life of the driver. Although there is some sign that
we are turning towards more respect for life than for
the things that destroy it, it is still hard to imagine the
confiscation of property as a penalty for ill manners on
the road.

Societies are all diseased with the sickness of acquisitiveness. Nations aggressively value their holdings and
their supplies of raw materials, especially if these have

any importance in the industry of war, such as oil or chromium, rubber or mercury. Commodities are used as ulterior motives for hoarding wealth, preserving privileges or imposing aggression on a weaker neighbour. Competitive constipation seems to be the most exalted modern method of international behaviour. What we have we hold, and the policy of circulation is subservient to the protective barrier of every kind of tariff.

Money and Work

Of course the moralists of their own acquisitive expediency have got hold of work, and are quite sure that we should not live unless we work, because we 'ought' to work. Nowadays we do not work to live, but live to work; and it is usually assumed that since all must work, nobody would work unless it was forced upon them by economic necessity. If there is work to do and if we work hard enough, then we are paid by our employers a more or less living wage, which is regarded as a due reward for our good behaviour.

But what is this moralized necessity, and by whom is it ordained? Why should we work? What is this moral compunction which has forced a slavery upon mankind, far greater than that which we may safely assume was ever intended by the punishment meted out to Adam and Eve for their disobedience of Divine command? We know how David, when he is frightened, likes to pose as Goliath. We know how liable we are to identify ourselves with the enemy, seen or unseen, in self-defence. It looks as if we have further identified ourselves with that initial punishment of the necessity to work, in order to protect ourselves against it, so that work has become doubly labour in a process of work about work, and thus labour itself has become an infinite regress.

But there cannot be any virtue in unnecessary labour and we may well enquire to whose advantage it is that we should thus virtuously earn a dubious living. It is not difficult to see that there are those who have a larger share of life's advantages, protected by the laws of property in a condition of meritorious and legalized fixation. Then everyone 'ought' to feel sure that they 'ought' to have that which they possess, and no one 'ought' to take it from them for the sake of our security in such a system. But there are many others who, having very little, are assumed to be in the position of moral duty towards their superiors in possession, while they must be content to earn such limited wages as £3 or £5 or £10 per week. Millions earn a living, some make a living, but a lucky few make money.

Should we bring up our children thus unquestioningly burdened with the moral obligation of earning a living? It is very doubtful whether such bondage within a neurotic system should be so dutifully encouraged. Besides such *earning*, however, there are other ways of *making* a living, such as becoming a member of one of the honourable professions, which are not similarly burdened by the moral virtues of an exceedingly limited income.

But why not go still further in the race for acquisitiveness, and take advantage of the way in which society is organized? Why not simply and honourably make money? The recipe thus to take advantage of the order in which we live is very simple. We must never deal direct in any useful commodity, never deal in reality, never handle the goods themselves and never grow anything for the community. Instead, we must buy (preferably with borrowed money) goods which only exist on paper, and sell them to someone who does not want them, but who, like ourselves, is also engaged only in the process of making money. We must deal only in the imponderable, gamble with the unseen, and the commercial deity will pour enough gold into our pockets to please our most egotistic avarice. It is easy to make money if we go the right way about it, but that is not by making goods. Only money matters, and we must be middle men if we are easily to make good. Thus do both relativity and metaphysics prove their reality, even in a society which is organized according to the unseen laws of infinite regress.

Circulation

The alternative to a policy of conditional hoarding is one of unconditional circulation. We need to live and think in terms of pipes or tubes, not closed vessels; means not ends, mediators not possessors, movement not fixation. Such a change of heart demands a full conversion, and perhaps vessels must be broken (and hearts too), before we can find this more contrite spirit as the force within our lives.

Let us state the problem clearly. Circulation of all the necessaries of life is an essential condition either for the health or the wealth of society. The solution to the economic problem is as deep as life itself. The organization of society must be alive, and must obey the laws of life. The egotistic purpose of possessiveness and privilege is not enough; it does not pay in the long run, but involves us in greater dangers to our security than it was originally hoped to avoid. Life moves, and so must we, in common weal or woe.

Those things which are required for living must all live and move in circulation; they must not be hoarded. This must happen unconditionally, without any condition whatsoever being imposed to act as a brake upon the wheel. Such necessaries, in whatever order we may state the list, include among others, food and drink, love, air, sun, money and blood. The importance of money in this list is that it should stand not for itself as gold, but as the symbol or ticket which it really is, for use as a medium of exchange into any other aspect of more vital currency.

If life in a community were founded on such a policy of wisdom, there would be so much less to fear. There must be fear, and anxiety is a necessary condition of our living truly in suspense. But there need not be so much, where we can at least be sure of the wherewithal to live, both for ourselves and our families. The whole strain of life would alter, and we could live with some other motive than that of perpetual defence. Both work and leisure would afford creative opportunity, where labour was not forced by economic necessity. Relationship within a community would be less aggressive, where all could be assured of the right at least to the necessaries of life.

Circulation is a sterling word, deeply rooted in the law of life, where rhythm is supreme. But it is not infallible; all movement is not good, and circulation may

DIAGRAM 23

ETERNAL NOW

ME   Now

ALL   I AM

I through ME
Eternity   "   *Space-time*
Greater   "   *Less*
Past   "   *Present*
Parents   "   *Child*

be as negative as a vicious circle if the direction of it goes widdershins. Infinite regress is one form of circulation, and although we must be slaves to this law, whether we like it or not, yet there is rotation in this way or that, negative or positive, fast or slow. Life holds us in a thrall of balance, which is why it does not pay us to try to escape, for truly we cannot, however successful our efforts may seem to be for a time.

The speed of circulation may only measure the ardour of our efforts to escape. There has been so much movement during the last century; but how much of it has been in the direction of escape? Progress has been external, but we have lost our grip upon the unseen forces of life. The geni is out of the bottle and life has only become more terrifying. Scientific development has brought much added knowledge, but less power to control the forces which it has set free. We are spinning on the edge of the whirlpool, aware of impending crisis: it is no wonder that we ask for peace, to guarantee escape from the penalty of past misdeeds. It is characteristic of our minds that we should feel so sure that the cure of our disease should be by repetition of the process of the disease itself, namely, escape. This is our dance macabre, by infinite regress, of illusion about illusion, and escaping even from escape, in vicious circle.

The 'circulation' of the Press offers us the perfect paradox of vice, because it is the very stronghold of all fixers who would externalize; it is the central keep of false security, the keystone of the arch of arch-aggression. Ready-made opinions are offered out of ulterior motives; sensationalism is offered cheap to those who have almost lost the use of their senses; vicarious experience is presented without effort to muddle-headed missionaries in mental strait-jackets. All for a penny, at our ease and for our relaxation, in wanton dissipation. The Press is the power behind the throne of gold, fixing distorted values, robbing us even of the power to think; it is the unseen master of our times. We are thus educated into error by the circulation of that mixed sensationalism and perverted propaganda which is miscalled 'news'.

It is significant that we could not hope for so much for our penny were it not for the presence of advertisement; it looks as if these advertisers are really giving us something for nothing! We pay this price for our news, and are then prepared to air our views, which are roughly worth about the price we've paid. It has all been offered so innocently, we have proved our independence at the price of a penny paid, and so the public, thinking that it buys, is really sold. Ulterior motives find their wildest opportunity in the uses of advertisement, for everything is offered under the suggestion that it is best for the consumer, whereas it is the seller who finds it worth his while to pay so high a price for propaganda. It is always hard to think clearly, and the process of true judgment requires the responsiveness of independent feeling: but with the clamorous din of other people's purposive opinions circulated from 'Press' and 'hoarding', so great an exercise of self has become well-nigh impossible. We have become externalized, unreal, beaten into a kind of stultified submission, which we are daily persuaded is the condition that is best for us.

It is not only the Press, however, which has this effect. Our more general reading of literature is not free from this same criticism, if reading has been actuated by the motive of escape. It seems so harmless to read; but what if all this publication is for the ease of our escape? It is not then so harmless, but takes important place in the process of our infinite regress. It does not matter how well any work of poetry or prose may have been written, nor indeed how true it may be to life; if it is used as an escape from the painful pressure of fact upon our lives, or as a means of effortless, painless and vicarious experience, its effect upon the psyche is destructive because it is being wrongly used. The sickness of our times is expressed, as much as in anything else, in the vast volume of books which issue in seething publication. Although it may be harmless in itself, such literature becomes a dead weight upon learning and an endless incubus upon our capacity for growth. It is but another aspect of our habit of wider dissipation, and offers the readiest excuse for every empty idleness.

We are forgetting how to live in this variety of useless opportunities to disseminate the potential vitality which is the Self. By this process of escape by externalization, we only seem to expand by outer contacts, but while thus seeming to gain in experience, we may actually be losing the very power to live. Our life thus spent in the purpose of multifarious escape is centrifugal. This can in time lead only to death, or to a return to the deeper satisfactions of inward experience. This is the crisis of our times, and the question now as ever, is—which way?

Truth and Insanity

Are we quite mad? If so, who are those others whom we call insane? Here is an opportunity for some analysis, which is badly needed if we are to clear the ground of misunderstanding.

Obsessed so deeply with reasonable virtues, we are afraid of going mad, and yet there is no life without a little madness. Insanity itself is perhaps not so bad a thing as this perverse refusal to allow of movement in our lives. Terrified of the unseen, fixing as an escape from movement, we come to regard life itself as being the same as that insanity which seems so much to be feared. They are not the same, however, for there is a stability, a generosity and a courage about life, that should serve to differentiate it from what we so fearfully regard as madness.

What is truth? Although there is in fact no intelligible answer to this question, yet there are some things which can be said about it. First of all, it is relative, conditional, and 'in the circumstances'. Three-dimensional truth is relative to three-dimensional conditions, and four-dimensional truth is relative to four-dimensional conditions. If we make the mistake of comparing the four-dimensional with the three-dimensional, then the one seems mad and the other bad; yet both, under their own conditions, are true. We must not transgress those limits which these truths impose.

Experience by the medium of consciousness, egotistically limited and sensorially measured, being but a slice out of time, is three-dimensional. It appears concretely true, but is in fact so limited a truth as to be but transient illusion or abstraction. If this is all that

249

Science knows, then Science, with all its accurate labour, can be but master of the ceremonies of death
because it can only rule over the inanimate. Within
these limits, science, reason, consciousness, the senses,
may all be true; but not for life, where circumstances
move and conditions swiftly change.

If society is to be arranged according to a three-
dimensional technique, it is put into a prison called
'the normal', 'the truth', 'the best', there to be fixed;
until those living forces which still exist beyond can
work their will, bursting to destroy these frail bonds
which human fear has imposed upon them. If society
is to be alive, however, a function of relationship, then
it must be ordered according to a four-dimensional
technique, which is another matter. Living demands
a living method, if it is to be organized; and living
truth is four-dimensional, not accurate but growing,
not fixed but moving, not egotistic and separative but
universal and free of dogmatic morality, whether scientific or religious.

If we are to live, then it is the virtues of courage and
generosity that are of most account, and we have to be
prepared to face the possibilities even of insanity if we
are to be sane. It is no use protecting ourselves within
some false concept of sanity, and then being terrified
because life is showing signs of breaking loose. We have
to agree with danger, feeling fear, accepting tolerantly
and obediently the nature and manner of our discipline.

From the standpoint of three-dimensional scientific
accuracy or beneficent morality, this four-dimensional
truth appears, however, to be either:

TRUTH AND INSANITY

1. So obvious as to be unworthy of mention ('it's only common sense').

2. Unreasonable, contradictory or paradoxical.

3. Impossible.

4. Unmoral or immoral.

5. Insane.

Yet within its limits, under conditions of growth, and in the circumstances of life, even so it may be true.

There are thus these two main classifications of truth, according to the conditions of X 3 or X 4, untimely or timed, fixed or moving, accurate or growing, sliced or whole. Each in its place, we need them both to live. It is no use to become abusive, in terms of mad or bad; as ever, the truth is within the inclusive conjunction 'and', not the separative and discriminative 'or'.

There are two truths, one moving and one fixed. Within the three-dimensional system we are dealing with that which is only true within limits and within specified conditions; it is a slice out of the living reality of truth. This fallacious cross-section, however, originates within the reasonable process of our own minds, and it is not easy to unlearn the false habit of believing in the evidence of our own senses. This is not the truth, this is only an aspect of it. This is not 'it', this is but a way of looking at 'it'; and every item of information which we have so painfully acquired as good, fixing it as moral or normal, has to be revalued according to the point of view from which it has been obtained. If it has been obtained by reason, then it is only reasonably true. In our experience there is so much of paradox that we must admit that reason is at least as often wrong as right, and that there are better ways of coming

DIAGRAM 24

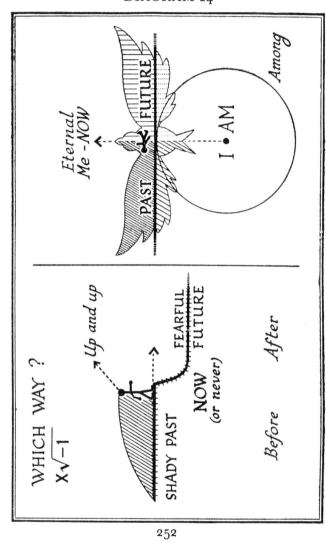

252

to conclusions than by the pessimistic process of always being right.

Truth regarded as a whole, including the other side of paradox, moving and fourth-dimensional, has to face many criticisms from the point of view of three-dimensional reasonableness. It may seem somewhat mad, but there is is. Surely to live we must allow ourselves to be a little mad, although not quite so mad as we become when we assert obsessive rights to fix our egotistic privileges. There is madness—and madness about madness, which is madder still.

Can we perhaps classify insanity? Fear of madness is with us all, but if we need a little of it, it would help us if we could know better which one we need, and which we can well avoid.

1. Successful identification with the world of X 3, usually called 'the normal', may well be a mask for insanity, where the infinite regress is being practised in perpetual escape. In a mad world, the insane will appear sane, and the sane insane. Even insanity is relative; and, for the matter of that, so is the treatment that is required to make us sane.

2. Where fixation is partial and unsuccessful, the perfect system of so-called normality becomes disorganized, with symptoms of minor mental disorder. There are cracks and loopholes of escape, evidences of instability, symptoms such as phobias and obsessions. None of these is so convenient and successful in its escape from the unseen, however, as the uncrackable system evolved under heading (1).

3. In the condition which we call insanity ('psychosis'), the system has broken down altogether. There

is none of the familiar order of X 3 to contain or control the forces which are in life X 4. It is important to realize, however, that there is a possibility that these people may have more latent powers of living than those who live so successfully and contentedly under system (1). Intuition, for instance, when driven into a pen by a strictly three-dimensional competitive educational system, may thus be driven mad.

4. Four-dimensional sanity transcends the limits of three-dimensional reason and normality. It is arrived at after having passed through much experience of suffering and accepted crisis, in which the old order has passed away. The subject has become reborn, converted, turned topsy-turvy, and thus has learnt eventually to abandon himself to the unseen. Such a one has let himself go, has felt a bit mad at times, and has sometimes been called so by those sure fixers who have so far lacked the courage or opportunity to share his experience.

It is all a matter of our attitude to life, part or whole, selecting or abandoned, egotistic or universal, protecting privilege or unconditionally sharing, having or being. Some children must-have privilege and protection; others are themselves, and wonder. It is these latter who hold the key to the fullness of their inherited kingdom.

CHAPTER VI: WISDOM

SUMMARY

Dreams.

Crisis. Two tides; aggressiveness and universalism; the contracting and expanding self; living in relationship.

Dimensions. Definitions and examples; four-dimensional experience; significance of Time; contrasting X 3 and X 4.

Words. Meanings change, X 3 and X 4; the error of dictionaries; 'Logos' and 'Maya'.

Free-will. Will or won't? Illustration of the jellyfish; the paradox of accepted discipline. I am; I will.

Old and New. Buddhism and Christianity; the error of our knowledge; the loss of deeper meanings.

Way of Life. X 3 and X 4 contrasted; hoarding and circulation; the teaching of Zen; 'I am that' and 'I am not that'. Education and the reversibility of Truth; Compassion.

Intuition. The age of forty; rebirth; the female aspect of the psyche; from intellect to intuition.

Three Men. Different attitudes to self and to experience; a matter of time; the fact of eternity emergent NOW.

WISDOM

The Tempest. The psychological moment and the tempestive now; common sense; luck; magic; the child who inherits.

Conversion. Jesus and John; 'in spite' and not 'because'; the meaning of love; the orchestra of life.

DREAMS[1]

XII. '*Up and Down*'

(a) I was in port on a ship, when a tremendous wave hit the side. My mother was on board and I said to her: 'Oh! dear, we have got to go out into the Atlantic tonight and meet some more of those!'

(b) I was looking up at a very high horizontal bar, which seemed to be suspended in the air. Someone was doing gymnastic tricks on it and I knew that it was my turn next. First of all I hung on by my hands, which did not feel so bad, but then I knew that what I had to do was to turn upside down and hang on by my feet.

I felt in an agony of terror at the bottomless abyss below me.

(c) I was walking on a narrow suspension bridge, only wide enough for one, which was very high in the air. I noticed in front of me the figure of a woman, and before I could do anything to stop her, she suddenly jumped over the side and I saw her twisting and turning through the air until she finally fell into the mud at the bottom far down below. I thought it was a pity

[1] For comment, see Appendix (page 307).

256

that it was not water, but perhaps being mud it might still be soft enough to save her. However, she seemed to have made just a small round hole in the surface and to have gone so far down that I felt she could not possibly live.

As I looked down, I had the strongest possible impulse to join her, but refrained.

(d) I was sliding down a terribly steep mountain side, digging my feet into the sticky clay in order to prevent falling into the river which lay below. I was with somebody who seemed to be leading the way and eventually we got to a part of the cliff which was quite perpendicular, but the girl I was with found what seemed to be a trapdoor with a piece of rope down which we could scramble to the shore below.

Here we found a house in which a lot of people were discussing doing something, one woman in particular being very discouraging and implying that it was always quite impossible to do anything.

Meanwhile, a boatload of people were waiting on the river outside, calling out to me and expecting me to join them, but I was not sure what to do.

(e) I saw an old man on a raft, which was almost submerged by the swift current.

I leapt on to the raft, and together we swept down the river between high banks and overhanging trees.

Chapter VI

WISDOM

Crisis

The rising tide of events presents our day and generation with a problem of vast crisis. Which way will this tide turn? Shall we be overwhelmed by the stress of these forces that we have lost beyond control, or shall we be drawn safely back to harbour once again, thence to sail the uneasy ship of Self on deeper and more tranquil waters?

There are two tides now visible, their effects on either hand. On the one hand there are ranged the overwhelming forces of aggressive nationalism, in which power is in the hands of destructive and dictatorial defenders, who zealously pursue their purpose. On the other hand there is a softer and a gentler current, represented by those who may be called the 'constructive-universalists', who on all sides and in so many different places and ways are seeing the deeper message of the unity of life. They may be unseen, unheard, they are not organized; and yet they live in multitudes, waiting in wonder and no little pain at the movement of events.

Wherever we look at the present day, these two forces are strongly represented, negative and positive, disruptive and creative, egotistic and universal, noisy and quiet, warlike and peaceful. We stand between these two poles, in opposite dilemma, drawn this way and that, with enthusiasts offering cheap salvation by one label or another to tempt us from some clearer path. Political missionaries advertise the moral benefits of their particular prejudices, as if there are so many different ways, each better than another, by which we can exercise the apparent privilege of our own free-will.

At the same time, however, there is this other process in the development of mankind, suggesting that the time has come for abnegation even of this vaunted privilege of free-will itself, substituting in its stead a policy of suffering and creative restitution, of being overwhelmed if needs must, rather than escaping from this dilemma of our circumstances. In these circumstances, is it any use to cry for peace as an escape? Peace is not a way of having, but of being. It must be accepted as an attitude to be adopted amidst the various appeals to resort to war for egotistic benefit of one kind or another. There is no Heaven except that obtained within the self, through resolute acceptance of disconsolate Hell. There is no lasting peace except by means of suffering within the self, internalizing those outward conflicts and so resolving them at last into their potential and initial unity, I AM—at peace amidst these powers, positive, sensitive, myself. Wherever we are set this problem of dilemma, with the possible solution by doing this or that in order to have peace, there is this other way of being peaceful, even amidst the strife of war.

In physics and philosophy, in science and in religion,

in psychology, art and in education, there are individuals (not only in this country but all over the world) who are seeing the possibility of this expansion of the self into the larger universe, by the acceptance of the whole nature of experience, expressed within the warring poles of such duality. It is characteristic amongst these modern representatives of the brotherhood of man, that they realize that all must be included in one embrace of general acceptance, without selection and without rejection, if the problem of our life and time is to be solved. Although this tide is not so noisy or ambitious as that other one of egotistic nationalism, yet it stands for the positive and creative aspect of our dilemma. It is not less strong because it may be less obvious than the noisy advertisements of the apparently greater and more efficiently organized forces of egotism and aggression.

There is a way of living in relationship that we have not yet fully discovered, either in ourselves or in society. It is quite simple, however, and depends upon the use of the conjunction 'And' instead of 'Or'. Even such simple words as prepositions are helpful to us in solving the complexity of our dilemmas, e.g. that we may discover freedom 'to' instead of freedom 'from', and freedom 'through' instead of freedom 'in'.

Such is the essence of what is described in the course of this book as 'four-dimensional experience', where growth is recognized as movement, and life as deeply rooted in the force of love. To live according to this law, however, we must both recognize and tolerate the supremacy of the unseen. We must live out of our depth, if thence is to arise the means of our salvation.

WISDOM

Dimensions

If we are to be so far out of our depth, then perhaps the best of all verbal plunges is into the 'fourth dimension'. But, rapidly for those who need a raft, let us make it with these commonplace materials. Our first point of reference may be that the moment we get off the thing we are on and look at it, we have introduced another dimension. The observing eye will thus always add one more dimension, or necessary measurement, to 'it'. We can have as many as we like for convenience, but for either wholeness, decency or courage, we must have at least four. Secondly, the fourth dimension may be said to include 'it' plus 'time', i.e. not only 'it', but also its growth or movement. Thirdly, the conjunction 'and' will let us into much of the secret; namely, that where 'It Absolute' is three-dimensional, 'It Relative' is four-dimensional. In other words, we must not forget that 'it' possesses a capacity to change according to environment, and we cannot afford to ignore this fact if we are to keep an eye on 'it'.

If it were possible to choose any other word than this, it could be taken with advantage, because there is a forbidding tone about this word 'dimension'; and also (like all others) it can be used in many different ways, with greater or lesser accuracy. It means a way of measuring, and that is a function of mind itself (Lat. *mensura*—measure, *mens*—month). It is therefore closely related to the whole experience of time; and it seems reasonable to use this word, in spite of its disadvantages, to express a difference in the attitude towards life which is so largely determined by our attitude towards Time.

262

DIAGRAM 25

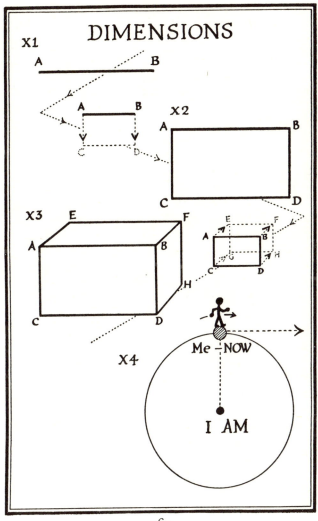

DIMENSIONS

X1

A ———————— B

X2

X3

X4

Me — NOW

I AM

263

Other illustrations of more concrete kind will follow, but meanwhile, in order to gain some further element- ary mastery over the meaning of this unpleasing and comfortless word, attention is drawn to Diagram 25, which suggests another aspect of multi-dimensional measurement. If a point moves along a line from A to B, it has traced out a 1-dimensional track, if this line moves at a right angle from AB to CD, it has traced out a 2-dimensional track, or plane surface; if this plane surface is moved again through a right angle to itself, it has traced out the volume of a cube, which is 3-dimensional; and if this cube itself be moved or spun or swung, its movement has given it a 4-dimensional reality. We can have as many dimensions as we please, by adding the eyes of our observers, and complicating the system of planes, using them as may be convenient for the measurement of our experience. The point is that we must have at least a measurement of four di- mensions, if we are to include the whole of that experi- ence of life which is represented by our movement in what we choose to call 'time'.

That aspect of a multi-dimensional system which is obtained in the infinite regress of the observing 'I', is the metaphysical process which led Dunne to describe phenomena in terms of the 'Serial Universe'. It is not, however, a limitation within the universe itself, but only a limitation in regard to our metaphysical attitude towards it. We can use this attitude if we find it useful, but we are not bound to do so unless we choose.

For four-dimensional experience, then, it is necessary to introduce these three concepts:

1. That the observer must be detached from, at the

same time that he functions in, the phenomena of his observation. This holds good whether these phenomena are external reality, or the inward medium of his mental or sensorial process.

2. The attitude of the observer to the nature of his experience must be positive, accepting it and not negatively rejecting it.

3. There is an unseen bondage, a reality of experience or 'being' implied by this attitude of accepted relationship, which, introduced by means of the Time factor, is the essential aspect of four-dimensional experience.

'Detachment from' implies 'movement in relationship with' this function of some unseen 'Time', and this provides the force for growth, which is the very essence of the vital principle. So small as these conjunctions are, 'Or' means aggressiveness and death, but 'And' means life. There can be no growth where any false identification has taken place between these two poles of opposites, such as for example male and female, or where they choose to set about each other in intolerant disharmony. Male and female, you and me, good and evil, light and dark, life and death, in each opposing couple the 'and' in this position has the significance of life.

It can easily be understood that we must have forced ourselves into some disadvantage and misunderstanding, if we have been trying to measure the greater aspect of truth by arbitrary reference to the limited standards of the lesser method of sensorial or conscious experience. Consciousness is a three-dimensional limitation of experience, cutting across the time track of our larger lives at an arbitrary point called 'now', in such a way that experience is presented to us as 'something plus time', instead of as 'something in time'. Conscious mind cannot by any of its mechanical methods appreciate the larger universe in which it finds itself, unless it is prepared to introduce itself willingly into the unknown, whether that be visible and tangible or abstract and metaphysical.

The world of our familiar experience is that of 'Science', which as an external reality is conveniently static so that it can more readily be measured. In it we use our senses, acquiring 'information', storing in memory or classifying in categories a mass of data, which are then filed for reference, or separated as unrelated 'it's' or absolutes. All such 'it's' are three-dimensional fictions; and as an example of a 'something', any concept either of the 'Unconscious' or the 'Conscious' by itself is as much an error of the three-dimensional thought process as consciousness itself can be.

A four-dimensional system of thought always recognizes reality as a function of relationship. It therefore includes all that contains life, the whole truth about anything, however small; music, movement, the self, the universe, from smallest part to largest whole. A list of four-dimensional words includes these: peace, love, joy, acceptance, suffering (which is 'acceptance', but not that protest which we know as pain), vision, prayer, feeling, meaning, breathing, balance, relaxation, co-operation, becoming, eternity, spirit, the universe, the self, the whole, life, death.

Apart from consciousness, which is three-dimensional,

we have many opportunities for appreciating a deeper awareness of four-dimensional reality. The statement that 'I am in Me Now', implies the presence of the larger in the smaller self, and also implies that we have a four-dimensional representation in the three-dimensional reality of any timeless abstract 'now'. In fact we are four dimensional beings in the process of becoming Now. (See Diagram 23, page 245; 'The Eternal Now'.)

It is important to notice how subjective time changes from that objective clock by reference to our own feelings. A change of mood effects a change in our sense of time. When we are happy time goes quickly, but when we are sad or in pain it goes more slowly, which might suggest some justification for a pessimistic attitude towards life. All it implies, however, is that our sense of subjective time changes with subjective mood, which again proves the four-dimensional nature of reality. It has been our general habit to regard both sleep and death as unimportant space, painful gaps, useless dustbins; but from the point of view of four-dimensional experience, these are now to be regarded not as limitations of reality (which is the function of consciousness), but instead as a far wider extension of it. Thus with change of viewpoint, the values change from minus to plus, as if we have been standing upon our heads in three-dimensional reality, and require to turn upside down again before we can enter into the wider realms of four-dimensional experience.

Those who are experienced in dream interpretation know some of the evidence for this deeper wisdom resident within the self, as I in Me. The phenomena of dream states introduces us to the realms of universal experience which transcend the limitations of time, and are open to those who are not so prejudiced by consciousness as to be unwilling to give up the arbitrary limitations which its method imposes. Four-dimensional experience of any kind, however, has been regarded with some suspicion, and very rightly so, because in the past it has usually been exploited to their advantage only by those who wished to make profit out of it. It is quite certain that four-dimensional experience should be approached with caution and with deep obedience to its laws. Seeing that it is so vast an expansion of human powers, there will always be those who want to use these powers aggressively, and who want to obtain them out of unlimited vanity and without expense or effort. Therefore it may have been wise to make fortune-telling and acts of prophesy illegal, although there may be no doubt as to the actual possibility of such experience. For those who are minded to be curious, however, we may well ask whether an Africa which believes in magic, or a Middle Ages which believed in witchcraft, were so mentally dark as our much vaunted Western civilization which, while professing to believe in neither, made them both illegal.

The timeless flash of intuition, the changing moods from depression to ecstasy, sleep and dreams, death (and also life), all provide evidence of four-dimensional experience, despite the arbitrary intrusions of consciousness to say 'That can't be true!' Yet there are many other evidences of further deeps beyond, in so-called 'extra-sensory' or 'supernormal' phenomena, especially those associated with trance states. There are ways of healing by suggestion, hypnotism, or faith, included under the harmless but suggestive word, 'influence'. Telepathy and telekinesis, clairvoyance and clairaudience, psychometry and prophecy are not the provinces only of quacks and charlatans. They are the happy hunting ground of life itself, for those who are prepared to die as well as live, lose as well as gain, in deeper circulation with the sense of life.

Can we now see more clearly the limitation upon experience which is imposed by consciousness, as it cuts with its insistent knife a slice through NOW? This consciousness is as three-dimensional as the reality which is presented for its experience; it has no sense of time apart from yesterday, today and tomorrow, so that it needs the external clock which hangs upon the wall, for all convenience of relationships, and to facilitate the catching of trains.

Our five senses are various ways of seeing or touching that timeless space in which we live, from which we can acquire 'knowledge' by a process of three-dimensional measurement, storing it as memory, to be coldly static in some pocket of the mind. The body, with its sense of unrelated self and false interpretation of experience as isolation and separation, is also part of this false interpretation of four-dimensional reality through the medium of three-dimensional phenomena. All experience is inclined to present itself in terms of unrelated 'its' as absolutes, like that false sense that 'I am absolute', too. Therefore this sense of aggressive egotism is due to the error of the medium by which we live, and the only way by which we can approach larger experience is by prefixing it with the contradictory statement: 'I am not only this, but I am also that.'

This vital way of living in relationship is the card of entry into four-dimensional experience, without which we are merely falsely identified with circumstance, as the watcher in the cinema would be if he saw himself only by identification with one character on the screen. The watcher in the cinema can give a good illustration for this need to be detached; our sensation is so much more keen and experience more enjoyable, if we can but assume that we are the beloved hero of the screen. Yet this method of false assumption, 'I am that', costs too great a price, because by making it we lose the values which we hoped to gain. Life loses reality, man loses freedom, mother loses child and husband loses wife. For acceptance of reality in larger sense we shall perhaps be called upon to lose our ideals and our favourite prejudices (the comfortable presence of a well-upholstered last ditch), but for what we lose in egotistic mask of so-called personality, we may gain in developed capacity for universal experience.

We can now place some equations of relationship between four-dimensional and three-dimensional experience:

$$X_4 = X_3 + \text{purpose, aggressiveness, movement,}$$
life, spirit, time, morals, or God.

i.e. for those who dwell only in a three-dimensional world, all those other concepts are necessary in order to make life seem true to itself. For those whose experience has led them more deeply and widely into life, there is no need for any one of those words, except to explain thereby the inadequacy of three-dimension-

al explanations of reality. Another equation states:
Reality = 'Science' + 'religion', where both must be
false, since each is less than true.

To summarize this difficult matter, let us place X 3
and X 4 side by side, in opposite columns, to see them
better thus opposed in their relationship:

X 3	X 4
I think	I feel
I ought	as if
to do	I want
Use, have, or do	Becoming, being, sharing
Emotion, thinking (conative)	Feeling, thinking (cognitive)
Instinct	Intuition
Conscience	Guilt
Perceptual, literal	Symbolic
Sensory	Extra-sensory
Identification (subjective)	Detachment (objective)
Hoarding	Circulating
Vessel	Broken vessel, tube
Square	Circle

There is another group of words which require
watching with especial care because they can occur
on either side of this list. They include Mind, Self,
Love, Peace, Judgment, and are all of deepest importance for the clearness and depth of our understanding.
Yet according to X 3 or X 4 their meanings may vary
as between antitheses. Thus words may either let us
down or blow us up, and yet within themselves be true.

Words

But perhaps in fact all words are capable of being
used three-dimensionally or four-dimensionally, and if
so, how can we distinguish between these two methods

271

of their common usage? The answer is that the three-dimensional use of words is by their accurate definition, which is a necessary and valuable method of employing them up to a point; it has the disadvantage, however, of being static, so that thus they can have no life. On the other hand the four-dimensional use of words has that advantage which accrues to art by giving life to meaning through allowing it to move. In spite of the disadvantage which may seem to belong to such laxity of expression, living words can no longer be such fixed and accurate absolutes, as they seemed to be when arranged in orderly fashion in the dictionary. Upon the page they leap to life, moving their meanings according to the way in which they are related—noun with adjective, adverb with verb—and according to how they are placed upon this growing stem of the sentence, which is so living, rooted on the page.

Grammar is in fact a vehicle of life, a means of circulation, but it can so easily be reduced to absolute dust by the accurate but reiterative misuse of its parts of speech by pedagogues on pedestals. Even handwriting tells the story of the mind behind the pen, and there is both art and science in calligraphy, if it has not been made more dead by those fixed forms of stylized script which are still taught in schools. Words are not such fools as those who use them, thinking they can be made to mean just this, when really within the word itself there are two poles far distant and quite opposite, between which each word lives.

Take for example the word 'temper'; it implies in steel the very essence of all discipline, yet in another sense, as it is applied to personality, indiscipline. The link is 'temperament', and so the word may be used as meaning either well or ill; well in the case of tempered steel, but ill for those who are 'ill-tempered'. (The deeper key to those who understand is Time.)

Two important words in this connection are LOGOS and MAYA, which each deserve especial attention because they are particularly fruitful illustration of this movement of meaning between the poles of difference. At one extreme of the line of meaning, the word LOGOS stands for the indwelling spirit, unseen and undefinable, the essential quality of meaning before it has been meant or framed in form, the light within the lantern. At the other extreme however, it stands for 'the word' within which that meaning has been incarcerated, for the lantern which has now become the vehicle of light for worse or better. Between these two poles our words must live, and stand there for our measure.

This leads us to the other word MAYA, which is an ancient Sanskrit root, having the same double meaning. On the one hand, it refers to a process of being in a state of measurement (expressed also in the Chinese word TAO), essential 'is-ness' in a state of balance or living in tune, time and rhythm; there is here an unseen quality, undefined and undefinable, and yet the essential unseen life of 'it'. But the form in which this 'it' presents itself to our experience, through the medium of sense and consciousness, is also called MAYA. But now it means 'illusion', i.e. we are now dealing with the three-dimensional projection or abstraction in terms of time, of that same meaning which in another sense is timeless and eternal.

Thus we may need dictionaries where words have so much complexity of meaning, but they are never to be relied upon as modes of fixing for our convenience, or meanings will be dead. It is obvious that anxiety, which is always thinking towards more convenient fixation, will morbidly hide itself within the covers of a dictionary if it can, instead of experiencing life at first hand where meanings live.

Language is living history of the movement of men's minds, and words of one time change their meanings at another. The simple 'fool' of medieval days was one to be congratulated alike for his simplicity and his foolishness, for he was a very child in truth. But not so today, where we are more exacting. 'Common' has also moved across the scale of values from praise to blame; but 'peer' has moved up, from 'equal' to 'above'. Yet still our words betray us, for speaking in love we innocently say 'My child, my pet'; while in more exasperated mood, we also ask, 'Why are you so childishly petty?'

Free-will

Here is a word to tax the freedom of our choice of words: free-will. Of all the problems that assail the mind, what can we answer to this question of free-will? Have we, or have we not? Referring to experience, as we have a right to do, it seems as if both these are true: not either, or—but and.

First, let us make a positive and negative analysis. What we mean by free-will is both the right and ability to change external 'it', according to our choice, i.e. the right to live aggressively. Accurately stated, this means not 'Free-will', but 'free-won't', for it is negative, and implies our right to argue and reject. Positively, free-will is quite another matter, and denotes an attitude of full acceptance of things as they are. 'Yes, I will,' expresses a willingness to answer to a call, accepting such discipline as may be imposed by circumstance, so that life becomes both a vocation and an adventure, through our obedience to a higher law. Thus has this word also turned upon us, and has shown, through paradox, its other face.

Perhaps an illustration by dimensional difference may also help to make our meaning clear, because the abstract must always have a concrete illustration.

A jelly-fish swims within its three dimensions, according to its choice; we may assume that it also feels itself blest with this fundamental right to exercise free-will. But the tide rises and falls (dimension 4) and a current sweeps it round the point (dimension 5). The jelly-fish is cast upon a shore, which doubtless comes as a surprise, because that was quite beyond his own intention. Upon the shore there stands a watcher with observant eye (dimension 6), who walks to and fro (dimension 7) stepping upon or avoiding the poor jelly-fish's corpse, according to his free-will or choice. The earth spins upon its axis (dimension 8) causing it to be time to return for dinner. The earth also rotates round the sun (dimension 9), the universe expands and swings in space (dimension 10).

That should be enough to show the limits of apparent choice; we have apparent choice within our own dimensional system, upon its plane, but not on either side or beyond it. But this is not much free-will. It is only an illusion, with apparent freedom to choose in these circumstances, surrounded by limits, deeply emphasized.

We are left with a paradox, that discipline is the only true way of freedom. We are possessed of freedom by virtue of our losing it; multi-dimensional free-will moves within the limits of a perfect discipline. I AM; and as I am, so I accept every limitation that forms part of my inward or outward circumstance. This requires a state of being in complete detachment, especially detachment from my own uncurbed desires. This may seem to be in fact the complete abnegation of all rights to choose, an abject slavery; but a positive attitude of willing acceptance to every negative that calls for discipline is the most that is left for us of our cherished right aggressively to change. I AM; but there are no words that can describe this state of freedom, and that is why all descriptive argument must fail further to enlighten this matter of free-will.

Old and New

In the process of development over thousands of years, the human mind has turned from a direct four-dimensional perception of experience to the extreme accuracy of three-dimensional perception which we call scientific knowledge at the present day. Men used to know by direct experience and intuition, but now we know another way, with partial and external accuracy. Buddhism was a system of four-dimensional empiricism, standing for Science in the highest sense, but like all religious systems it became incarcerate in the prison of a philosophic commentary. Christianity died within its Christian church, in crucifixion following its founder. Mathematics, originally a philosophy, has become a method of balancing accounts, buying and selling, building houses, or judging the movements of the stars. The language of the ancient Jews contained its own religion, complete in a living system for those who understood, and has probably never been surpassed for scientific accuracy in its power to weigh and measure four-dimensional experience. It is very doubtful, however, whether there are many Jews of the present day who have this deeper sense of the value of their ancient truth.

Today we live in consciousness, unfriendly to the unseen. Our world is mechanized, externalized; we no longer seek to live within ourselves. The power over matter which we have gained by added knowledge is waiting to destroy us with bigger and better guns, deadlier gas, faster bombers from the air. The enemy is at our gates, and gates are everywhere.

We have gained a vast store of knowledge from this capacity to deal with the seen aspect of experience, but neurosis will run wild into insanity if we continue to lose sight of deeper meanings and the law of larger movements. Like the passengers who continue happily to dance on board some vessel whose side has been irremediably shattered, we do not know the fate which soon awaits us. The panic is not yet, because we do not understand how near we are to that Death, the reality of which we have so wildly fled.

It is not that this external aspect of reality contains anything which is necessarily wrong, nor is the illusion of MAYA itself to be despised. The pendulum has swung to its opposite side of error in those who class together the world, the flesh and the devil, as evil things to be eliminated. These are now with us, as an aspect of reality. Framed in consciousness and mirrored upon that three-dimensional screen, is the total essence of four-dimensional reality, which some men call God. It is only if facts are taken out of time and relationship that they become fallacies.

Organization of the unseen will blind us to the light, if our neurotic prejudice is in favour of the organization and fearful of the unseen. Thus the Church can become the greatest enemy of Religion, and schools of Education. The Law can become the very altar of aggressiveness, and Medicine can propagate every error of ill health, if it does not pay proper attention to the supremacy of the unseen, from which both life and healing come. Politics will order relationships by the egotistic arrogance of authority, losing all sight of policy and principle in the exalted enmity of evil manners. Organizations become even more efficiently organized, and big business fails to see how worthless and irrational the method of rationalization must become, unless it plays its part in obedience to the deeper laws of economics.

We have worked our way to the present situation of instability and unrest, and now at the point of crisis the question is, Which Way? Shall we be destroyed by the Frankenstein of our most rational and accurate creation, mechanized to perfection, or shall we let it go, dying unto the unseen? It looks as if the days of the old system are not only numbered, but outnumbered, and unless we can get back our obedience to deeper laws, we shall be swept away as other failures have been overwhelmed before our time.

OLD AND NEW

How simple to say: 'We must have peace!' How easy to advocate its virtues and talk of brotherhood amongst all mankind, how desirable simply and without effort to redeem all the errors that we have made, to live and never to die, to wake and never to sleep, to own and never to lose, to be absolutely King of an uncriticized Castle, where all the dirty rascals have been relegated to the bottomless pit of some invidious unseen.

We must have peace! But this word like all others is capable of so much mismanagement, that if we are to find its meaning it can only be by the process of detachment from it, being willing to lose that which we most wish to possess. Must-have peace is must-have war, because 'must-have' belongs to the policy of aggressiveness and defensive armaments. There is no must-have about peace, for peace is letting go, a policy of detachment, of objective discipline, a way of life which is not obedient to any arbitrary technique.

In order to achieve successful purpose, the three-dimensional method may seem to be direct, and thus may be successful for a time. If we only want to go from here to there, then let us draw a straight line and keep upon it; but the laws of four-dimensional logic contradict the apparently simpler laws of three-dimensional experience. Not thus by a straight line, but round and round, life moves. Children cannot be made to grow the better either by pushing or pulling. The method of impatient aggressiveness pays no more with children than it does with plants, as any gardener can tell us. In time, with much obedience, even that rare flower of peace may grow, but its existence depends upon a way of life: X 4, and not X 3, is the peace which passeth understanding.

The Way of Life

So let us classify two ways of life, according to this distinction between three-dimensional and four-dimensional methods:

	X 3	X 4
Personal Aims	Security, fixation and material progress	Culture, growth and wholeness
Manners	Anxious, artificial, aggressive	A very gentleman, occasionally overcome by spontaneous sincerity
Morals	Selective—rejective Causality Absolute	Total acceptance Balance Relative
Art	Copying accurately Escaping from both life and death	Creative imagination firing through disciplined technique. Life in being
Education	Knowledge dissociated, purpose material Memory for luck	Adaptability and creative insight Foresight
Science	Materialist and moralist Facts, not method	Empirical: total: the same method for both seen and unseen
Economics	Fixative, power through possession	Distributive: unconditional circulation of all the necessaries of life
Politics	Power; security by treaty and armaments: you *or* me: aggressiveness	The essential brotherhood of man, differently expressed and fairly treated: you *and* me

THE WAY OF LIFE

	X 3	X 4
Commerce	Cut-throat competitiveness and possessiveness	Co-operation and enough all round, including leisure
Philosophy	Dead	As large as life: the supremacy of the unseen: relative not absolute: inward not outward: moving not fixed
Psychology	Systematized	
Religion	Idolatry of the external Absolute. Externalized. Fixed in Church, dogma and creed	
The Norm	Paranoia: schizophrenia	Life more abundantly

The new way of life is therefore to act as tube but not possessor. The vessel of our incarnation must have suffered some damage in the course of its experience, however, before it can appreciate the higher nobility of 'a broken and a contrite heart'.

It has been the particular teaching of Zen Buddhism that consciousness must be transcended in order to approach the deeper levels of religious experience, and for this purpose was devised the method of 'Koan' to tease the anxious accuracy of smaller minds. Problems were set like unanswerable riddles, yet answers were demanded. Stories were told which were obviously ridiculous, and the mind was held in a vice until it gave up all such idle questioning, hopeless and in despair. Zen does not permit any mental attachment to the simplicity of visible accuracy, and Zen is thus true to the state of paradox which is life.

It does not seem necessary, however, to resort to the artificial discipline of such a technique in order to demonstrate the polar opposition of our experience. We are too anxious for an answer to life's problems, seeking for the false simplicity of this or that, where in fact both are true. Such problems are in their very nature insoluble, and we are wrong in trying to solve them. We are only right when we accept the merits of each side, adapting ourselves positively to them both, regarding such a situation as a necessary if painful fact of life. 'I am these two and between these two I live'.

Thus the way of hoarding gives place to the less apprehensive process of circulation. Memory is here a danger, if it does but store; for some it is to be regarded as a habit of living in the idolatrous dustbin of the past, instead of in the expansive movement of a more vital NOW. Memory may offer infinite opportunity for escape. Yet tradition is not to be destroyed, for the past is true and is one living root of time. It is something, however, which requires to be expressed in the present, not as a fixed copy of the past but as its more vital child. Thus in suspense between the poles of yesterday and tomorrow, life and eath, I and Me, self and not-self, accepting the insolubility of life's problems, we still can say 'I AM', living or dying with equal grace in the rhythm of our time. (See Diagram 24, page 252.)

Awareness of the universal self, through the breaking down of those vast limitations of consciousness in the illusions of egotistic unrest, opens up a new and deeper store of life. We are not to say any longer: 'Thank God I am not as other men are', or 'There, but for the grace of God, go I,' but rather 'I am that man.' The meaning of all brotherhood is that: 'Whatever has happened or can happen to any other man, woman or child, animal, plant or thing, can also happen exactly so to

me.' The true possibility of vicarious experience is that
we should thus be prepared to take within the self, as
happening to Me, that which we would choose should
happen only to some other. This is the true practice
of acceptance, called 'compassion'; 'I am that', whatever 'that' may be and however painful. This has been
the practice of asceticism throughout all ages, but there
is no need to carry it to the extreme where it becomes
identified with masochism and thereby loses balance.
Not either, or, but both: always these two in their relationship. Both pain and happiness, each peacefully
accepted to deeper satisfaction; sickness and health,
each vitally loved; self and not-self, beloved enemies
to be treated alike with wisdom and compassion, yet
without any sense of false identification.

But balance demands not only 'I am that', but also
'I am not that'. This is the vital point to keep us true,
if we would be inclined to veer to one side or the other.
If we are inclined to false identification, then we need
to repeat to ourselves the other side of its balanced
opposite: 'I am not that, I am myself, alone, here,
now.' If on the other hand we are inclined to over-
simplify and ignore relationship, then the point to
emphasize is 'I am that', in order that it may be in-
ternalized within the self, and thereby added to the
self's experience in terms of universal brotherhood.

The truth is characteristically reversible, and is at
least as true the other way about. As proverbs show,
there is no statement of truth which cannot and should
not be contradicted by its opposite. This is again the
basic teaching of Zen Buddhism, and could be used
more fully in our educational method, if teachers were

less afraid of truth and less inclined to fix matters to some advantage.

To make thought move, and save it from fixation in the easier fallacy of absolute fact, all positive statements should occasionally be contradicted by their opposites, suggestively, provocatively and fearlessly. For instance 'I am not like that' requires the balanced opposite fact that also 'I am like that'. We should thus also teach the discovery of infinite importance that, in spite of simpler mathematics to the contrary, $2 + 2$ does *not* always $= 4$, because total value is also conditional upon the relationship of added parts, whereby the whole is greater than that sum. Similarly, though God is good, God also is not good; or at least not only good, for He is also True, and thereby transcends the limits of our small morality, including in Himself the whole of what we judge as good and evil. Proverbs thus tell the truth by contradiction, e.g. 'The longest way round is the shortest way home'. In the world of four-dimensional experience, where time is to be included, rhythmic curves may seem a long way round, but short cuts and direct methods do not pay. In fact, the obviously false may still be true; e.g. in spite of logic, the part may be greater than the whole. It is a mistake to be too particular in our efforts to understand such four-dimensional problems, but, for suggestion in this matter, there is some greatness implied in every seed that transcends the poverty of its parent plant.

Such statements in apparent contradiction to obvious reality are in fact the elements of wider understanding, the growing points of mind; but they must at times be forced upon us, in order to avoid over-simplification and undue aggressiveness about experience. In fact, the truth of life is balance. Yet how much of the effort and expense of education is spent in contradicting this essential truth? It is a one-sided, distorted and departmentalized affair, as if a part of life can be conveniently isolated, like some poor pinned butterfly. 'That is a life—that was!' So history may mar the truth, science murder fact, and religion build the altars of idolatry.

It is not enough to watch, for we must also feel. To see all, in infinite detachment, will effect but half a truth, if our heart is not contained in what we see. A little balance therefore counts more for wisdom than much knowledge. Science is not enough unless it has its heart in life; but neither can sentiment fulfil the role of accurate detachment. We need both head and heart, always engaged and always balanced, for any truth of life to be revealed.

Diagram 26 (page 286) illustrates the need for this duality, that we should both keep the eye detached, and yet at the same time never lose touch with the heart of the unseen. This is the meaning of the three word way: 'Watch . . . and pray.'

Of course we can escape from life by any way, and one will do as well as any other. The four-dimensional method may also be used as a means of escape from the reality of experience, which has led so-called 'mysticism' into some disrepute. True, it may be an escape: it never does to feel sure that our purpose is not avoidance of some pain. The watching requires to be endless, infinite. To live fairly we must live in the midst of our experience; seeing how we are in it, we must keep this

DIAGRAM 26

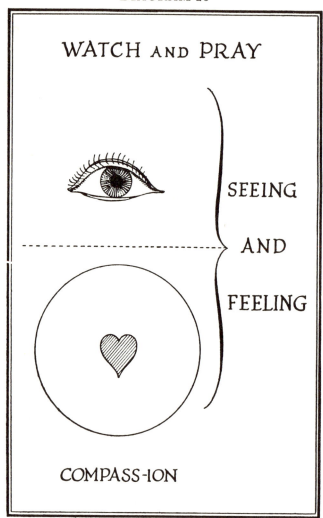

WATCH AND PRAY

SEEING

AND

FEELING

COMPASS-ION

cool detachment and yet never lose warm heart. The art of living is between these two, where science is inclined to overbalance on the one side, and religion on the other. Between these two we live; anything which leans to one side or the other is to that extent an error of the true technique of life, which manifests the wholeness of reality.

Intuition

There is a rhythm in the curve of life which finds at about the age of forty a deeper need to change towards this inward path. It is as if the earlier half of life must learn first how to live, before it can learn the larger truth of how to die. Material progress has reached its height, the family seed has been planted, position is assured and success can only look forward to eventual decline. This is the period of threatening depression, as advancing years offer no other hope than that of losing what has been so hardly gained.

This then is the period of potential rebirth, when the depth thrusts out its needs again, demanding a return to deeper things. Now is the time for successful aggressiveness to learn the deeper truth, as the other half of life comes forward for completeness, changing material progress to spiritual depth, instinct to intuition, male to female way of living, and death to rebirth. The change requires courage, but not that of aggressiveness. The instinct of aggressiveness is a man's cowardice, but intuition is a child's fact and a woman's courage, for a man to learn again as he becomes older.

It is the female aspect of the psyche which thus requires to be fulfilled in the rhythm of developing ex-

287

perience. First male, then female: first the experience
of the seen, then of the unseen: first waking, then
sleeping: first having and doing, then becoming and
being: first life, then death. It is as if we need the
recreative effect of some deeper inward dip, a way of
sleep, peace and letting go the tension of our fierce attachments, to be overwhelmed by our abandonment
into this reality of the unseen, which has been so long
neglected and so fearfully escaped. The change may
seem like death, where habits of living have been most
arbitrarily fixed: but this death is to be heartily em-
braced, this depression of the self is to be willingly
encouraged, forced even further down. The depression
which we experience with so much evidence of grief
is the outward proof of unwillingness to be depressed.
This is what in fact we need: to go down into the depth
of the unseen within ourselves, falling, abandoned,
overwhelmed—until we can be reborn, to wake, as if
to a new day. This is the time for change of attitude,
but so much past habit and poor teaching still bids us
to hold on.

From intellect to intuition: from storing to circulating: from personal to universal: from holding on to
letting go: from climbing to falling: from living to
dying: this is the crisis of life, and the crisis particularly
of our times. Can we let go, falling willingly—or must
we be shattered by the law of life, which demands inexorable obedience, soon or late? Delay makes matters
worse, and the role of healer is not to support this falling structure, crying some panacea of cure, but to play
the part of gynæcologist to death.

Intuition is the term which best describes this greater

288

wisdom, but it is a definable technique which requires some understanding of its laws. It is not only mystery and miracle, it is an experience of that reality which is very near the heart of life. It is not the privilege of some rare mystic few, it is the need and primary process of us all.

Children are intuitive: this is their key to the kingdom to which grown men may thus eventually return, sadder and wiser for their experience of the fruits of knowledge. The process and method of intuition are not new, but they do require the framework of a new metaphysic within which to take respected place. Sleep, trance, death: the ecstasy of life: guess-work and the flash of instant vision: the birth of a new idea: wonder and an inexpressible joy: these are for all, if the bias of unbalanced education in bitter competition with the truth has not entirely eliminated from experience the reality of the unseen.

Intuition is the direct method of experience, where that derived from sense and consciousness is not only indirect, but also limited, illusory and inaccurate. Consciously we live in part, within the limits of our senses, through the medium of 'space' and 'time', believing the measures of our senses to be true. Yet there is more in life than either sense or that which seems to be non-sense. Immediate experience is not negative, nor is it only illusory experience of the non-existent. Intuition is an unlimited insight into that mystery of self and life, which consciousness can only partly scan. Can Science add intuition to its technique of measurement of the phenomena of life, or is this faculty of insight to remain for ever beyond its scope?

WISDOM

Here is the place to outline a new metaphysic, a new hypothesis of self and life and universe, for Science to see if it can see, and still retain its self-respect.

The Three Men

Diagram 27 (page 291) must now tell its tale, describing what we mean of these three men. First we can see the Little Man, standing upon his track in time at some point NOW, with PAST behind (as 'memory') and FUTURE spaced in front as some faint hope. He lives quite sensibly, and feels that he is now. He measures life according to a three-dimensional metaphysic, however, for TIME is but the clock upon his wall, and he must beat it if he can. He lives urgently, aggressively, striving up and up, for hope is always round the corner, near or distant, but never completely within the limits of his grasping hand. His present is dogged by the panting breath of his past fears and unfriendly errors, so that it is sometimes hard to say whether he is the more anxious to arrive at his distant goal, or to escape from the unseen enemy who seems so large a figure in pursuit. Sometimes, in moments of successful ecstasy, he achieves the summit of desire: and then, his one ambition is to hold it all, against all comers, in case they might take it from him, for there cannot be enough to share, and enemies are numerous. His constant fear is that he might lose that which he has, which cannot be enough. So death must be his last and largest enemy.

But in course of time he grows to realize a somewhat larger scope of life and self, becoming Middle Man. He knows his past is true: his future also, though so

DIAGRAM 27

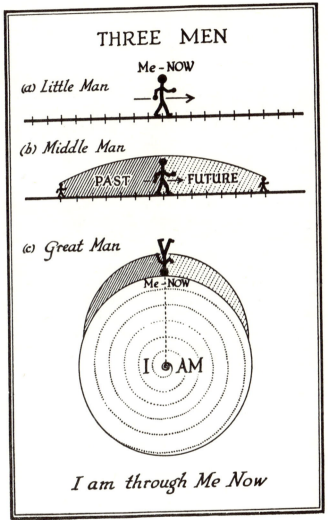

THREE MEN

(a) Little Man

Me-NOW

(b) Middle Man

PAST →← FUTURE

(c) Great Man

Me-NOW

I AM

I am through Me Now

much more dubiously dark. Yet in regard to both, from life to death, he still can say: 'Yes, I am that.' He sees his self no longer merely as a slice, but also as a sausage: as if each instant has been laid side by side in continuous close touch, to form this solid Self-in-time, from birth to death. Then this is Self: not slice, but sausage. Not this small part of Me-in-time, but all of Me, through time from birth to death, contains my Self, and is implied in the slice of time which we call NOW.

This sense of larger self is particularly important in regard to children, if this man is to be a teacher of the young. We are inclined to regard children merely as their little 'Nows', these little cross-sections which they present to us, not realizing that here is a process of becoming, an individual who contains in this seed 'now', so much of past, so much of future. We should look at children not as bodies of such an age, and minds of such a development, but as these long-shaped tubular sausages from birth to death, whole beings with past and future both implied. This makes the teacher somewhat smaller, however, and adds both to his responsibility and to his possibilities for responsiveness.

But having conceded so much to the unseen as to allow the reality of both Past and Future, we may now concede more, for there is not enough movement in our picture yet. Let us stand our Little Man upon his head, as one point upon the surface of a vast sphere (drawn conveniently small) extending his straight lines to join in vast infinity, with Past behind him, and Future spaced in front. This Middle Man is then but

one small arc of this great sphere: can we guess what
entered his beginning and left him at his end, giving
him continuity between the unseen and the seen? And
can we guess the relationship of circumference and
centre, or part to whole? As sleeping and waking,
rhythmic, so perhaps are life and death to some essential spirit, which passes out again after death to continue upon this devious whirl of various experience.
Perhaps, after all, the seen is thus conditioned by the
unseen, and the part is dependent upon the whole.

Poised as a point upon the skin of this Great Man,
we can learn much if we do but realize that Little Man
is habitually standing upon his head, seeing an inverted image of reality, projected from some deep unseen centre upon this moving screen of Now. It is not
'Time' that moves, but 'Now', which is a point upon
the surface of a rotating sphere. Let us imagine that
some ray of light has been shone from centre to circumference, its point of impact being this Now. Let us
imagine that this ray of light is in swift rotation, how
far and how swift we do not know, but covering vast
areas of space and time. Then (as in a train) the Little
Man, self-satisfied, will think that the countryside is in
movement, when actually it is himself that moves.

In such a scheme, Eternity becomes a fact, Past and
Future are as actual and as present somewhere as
This Now, but they are not present to the mind of
Little Man, owing to the limited focus of his consciousness, which is a moving point in Time. It is possible,
however, in dreams to detach ourselves from this point
of consciousness, thus adding to our experience of some
other space and time, travelling other time-tracks and

meeting other members of this our universal brother-hood. Trance mediumship, prophesy and dreams all belong to that larger science of this Greater Man's experience, capable by a more accurate metaphysic of being realized and somewhat understood, even if they must be still to some extent intangible.

The aim then of our experience is to express this Greater Man, the whole of Self, including in himself all people, all past and all future in this living present, 'I am in Me'. Then God, as reality not myth, is in 'I AM', (I am that I am). He is the all-inclusive whole, inexpressible and eternal, and yet expressed within the limited phenomena of our experience of space and time.

The Tempest

The difference between intuition and the more commonly recognized instinctive modes of experience depends entirely upon our attitude towards the unseen. It is not scientific to say that because it is unseen, therefore it is not there; it may be, and if science is to apply the laws and limits of its own methods, it must be exactly as friendly and positive towards the unseen as towards the seen. It must never select or choose, moralizing over the good and bad things of experience.

For example, the varied experiences of sleep can no longer be regarded only negatively as a waste of time or empty space. Facts are so simple sometimes that we neglect to notice them, but the fact about sleep is that this inward dip beyond the limits of consciousness has the effect of deepest recreation, so that we awake refreshed. It is as if we have experienced some deeper

flow of life, which we then spend and lose in consciousness, to regain it once more with the recurrent rhythm
of this space of sleep. Sleep is in fact not an empty space
and not a dustbin, as dreams will show. It is an extension of experience and not a limitation, and is in
close parallel with the related positiveness of the unseen
phase of death. The metaphysical concept of rhythmic
continuity is not an unverifiable hypothesis, but is one
of simple common sense, than which none better. It
can be proved by experience and is in fact proved by
everyone, both day and night.

Has it been made plain that there is more in life
than we are prepared to recognize, and that the in-
wardness of mystic experience is not the prerogative
of far-off saints? It is the truth about life for all to
experience, not by a process of departure or escape
from reality, but by a method of bringing it down to
the earth of immediate experience, expressing Eternity
within the limits of this space-time Now.

'Common sense' is the name we give to the experience of universal wisdom, which is shared amongst all
mankind, intuitive, true and unchanging. Perhaps
nowadays it is not so common as it might be, although
still deeply prevalent. There has been nothing in this
book beyond the limits of this 'common-sense' experience, not even the next diagram of the 'mind in
a whirl'. We have all had that experience at times,
when we have attempted to fix the movement of our
moving system against the grain of fact. The experience of the mind in a whirl is the end result of an
unsuccessful effort at fixation, but we whirl just as
much in mind, as does the world upon which we live

—and equally without knowing it. Science and physics know that reality is flux and should be able to demonstrate the better the fallacy of holding on. Like life, and reality, the Science of Self must move. My mind is in a whirl? Then let it be.

We live at the growing point of opportunity, yet so many of us live so superficially, so slightly and so selfishly that we do not realize the powers that dwell within us. We fail to express them in vital experience, because we are too fixed to take a chance by living in this adventurous 'Now'. We have a clumsy phrase 'the psychological moment' to express the presence of a time and tide 'which taken at the flood leads on to fortune'. Such fitness and adaptability, grace and responsiveness, balance and surrender to the movement of events, is surely what we mean by 'Luck'. But Elizabethan language had a better phrase, and called it the 'tempestive' moment (see Diagram 28, page 297), suggesting that our fitness, adaptability and grace depend not upon our capacity to alter experience, but to respond willingly and surrender to it. This should further prove again the fallacy of free-will, which is the error of the Little Man, who has not realized his limitations.

. . . . .

So this is magic, just to live; not trying to alter, with our egotistic sense of self-righteousness and determination, the errors of our enemies and friends. Is this all that we are to realize, that all is illusion and that not even the last ditch is to be defended against the overwhelming forces which rise up to threaten us with new movements and new time? Life is magic and it

DIAGRAM 28

THE TEMPEST

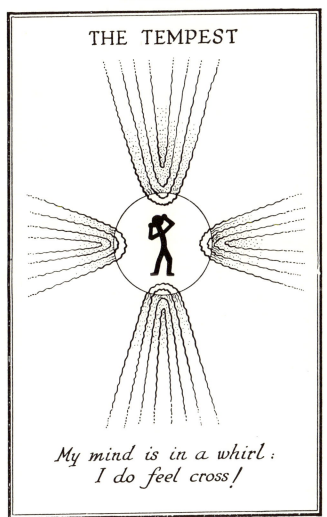

My mind is in a whirl:
I do feel cross!

leaves us so, presenting us with this changing cinematographic screen of infinite illusion for our experience. There are so many ditches and so many occupants, but there are none in which we can safely fix ourselves, whether religious or metaphysical, material or abstract. All is illusion; yet, as such, to be loved with inspired courage. There is greater love even than that of laying down our lives for a friend: it is that we should be willing to make this same sacrifice for our enemies also, even for the cause in which we do not believe, for love is truly unconditional.

This is the law of the child who inherits; that he should Be and not argue, that he should feel and not externalize, that he should live and not insist upon the betterment of his experience. This is the beatitude of Luck, which does not necessarily imply any painful fact of crucifixion, although of course this may be part of life's experience. There are those whose experience of it has been the other way and who by being present exactly at the time, gracefully, have never ceased to move, thereby enjoying the fullness of experience without too great a part to play of actual sacrifice.

There is no need to be morbid about the difficulty of this life in which we find ourselves, for there is no undue difficulty about it, if we will but realize that we bring the difficulty upon ourselves by trying to alter the inevitable. The Little Man is so afraid of being overwhelmed, but the Larger Man hopes for it; the Little Man refuses to swallow so much of his experience, regarding it as evil, but the Larger Man takes it as his everyday diet, keeping open pipe and open house for every enemy to pass through; the Little Man is terrified lest he should slip back from light into darkness, from seen into unseen, but the Larger Man realizes that it is but sleep or death and either is the very practice of his recreation; the Little Man depends upon 'goods' or golf for his well-being, seeking for doctors or other saviours, but the Larger Man knows by the deeper process of his inward conviction that truth is paradox and that he is safest when he is least defended.

Paradise regained is the acceptance of Paradise lost. The fullness of the flower of man's experience is to be, and give, as flowers. The level of our dependence is not to be found upon the same plane as that upon which we live. The cause is in the unseen and we are attached, as flowers are, by some invisible umbilical cord to that deeper soil from which we draw our sustenance. Neither food, doctors nor armaments, neither dictators, parents nor saviours, can really effect or establish our security. The cause is in the unseen, where the flower of being is deeply rooted.

Reality is the product of the intangible, a fruit of the unseen, an incarnation of the spirit. We may prove the contrary, but then the proof will be wrong, for we cannot prove the reality of the unseen, except by our experience of Being, and that must be enough for knowing. This is the predicament of Science, and illustrates again that life requires the double root of paradox, for so it lives.

Life, reality, being, must each be recognized as illustrations of a deeper peace, not needing change in spite of egotism's urgent desire for fairer privilege. The war of life is one thing: man's war is another, being war about war, war against war, in infinite regress of offensive and defensive argument. The way of peace cannot be more sure than that of war accepted, peace about war, difference agreed upon, tolerant relations amidst the moving stresses of opposing poles, rhythm and harmony. The music of the spheres is best expressed by this deep note, I AM. Let us be still about this movement, at peace about this semblance of an inward and outward strife, thus resolving paradox by accepting its duality with essential unity. Choosing, we must choose wrongly, if we would exclude either one or other source of our dilemma.

We may grumble about paradox, but there it is, part of the moving framework of our lives. Free-will is gained by fullest discipline, and largest life by losing this small self, this impatient self-conscious and material 'Me'. This is no more, in fact, than Being or Becoming, true to Self; and thus true to that larger universe, of which the least detail is truly mirror of the whole.

The real universe is a system of infinite evolution, and is mirrored in the life of man. We make it harder than we need and modern civilization is making of it a system of infinite regress, in argument about it and about. We need to stand the other way up, inverted or converted, if we are to realize this larger truth; turning No to Yes, rejection to acceptance, intolerance to tolerance, and thus all things to love. There is nothing that it is better for us to avoid: no, not even Death. There is nothing that it is not better to accept, even though it be the expression of our enemy's ill-will. There is no progress other than what is, if we would let it be: for all Eternity is in this Now, if we could but see and let it live, within and through this channel of the separate self.

Conversion

The most dramatic moment in the life of Jesus illustrates this common truth of Life, emergent, Now. Every instant of experience is an example of rebirth, through baptism by the water and the spirit, but few can realize the fullness of what this means, as Jesus did, and taught.

He heard that John was baptizing in the River Jordan, and went to him. John, naturally diffident, said: 'I have need to be baptized of Thee, and comest thou to me?' Jesus replied: 'Suffer it now: for thus it becometh us to fulfil all righteousness.' Then he suffered him and Jesus went up straightway from the water, and lo! the Heavens were opened unto him and he saw the spirit of God descending as a dove and coming upon him. (Matthew iii, 14-17.)

Drama or dream, religion or science, universal or personal, mysticism or common sense: this is true to life, it is the hidden law of our experience. Whether or not it may betoken the larger moment of conversion, this is the way in which life breaks upon us constantly, as inner food for being. The only difference is that, although in all it happens thus, some know of it in deepest recognition, and thus become converted to the way of its acceptance.

To live in this larger sense, converted, is to live 'in spite of' (i.e. notwithstanding) and not 'because': unconditionally and not conditionally, which is the true meaning of the word to 'love'. At first we may believe that, as 'Hate' is 'dislike' multiplied, so is 'Love' a consequence of 'like' much emphasized. But in this sense love is still as much conditional as like, and both will only do their work 'because'. Such is not love in truest sense, but the distinction, most necessary for our understanding, is one of a dimensional difference. For 'conditional' love is three-dimensional, but 'converted' love is four-dimensional, whole, holy and healed.

The effect of such an open pipe to life, expanding in opening circles so that the force itself may the more freely pass through us 'notwithstanding', is to gain in four-dimensional efficiency; for this is truly being, in the sense that flowers and children are, yet with the added knowledge derived from maturity of experience. Thus we may be established on both banks, as well as flowing with the river. We are balanced between two worlds, and yet thereby unified in a third reality of Self. In four-dimensional sense, this is the whole of life, in paradox, in picture and in truth. Thus we may prove in Being the universal unity of Life.

But in case this picture may seem over-simplified, and therefore incomplete because it does not allow sufficiently for the multitudes of men in their more complex relationships, let us add one more to the mixed bag of metaphor, and consider the orchestra which plays a composition under the baton of a conductor.

First, a polite assumption that our orchestra has an unseen conductor besides the visible one, a living, active ghost. A flight of birds wheel as if at an unseen command: a colony of ants go about their business as if each one is obedient to the higher law of its com-

munity: bees return to hive as if one moves according
to the will of many: the colonies of cells which form
the Self, through diversity of their relationship, create
a community which is under the leadership of conscious Me. Thus many make one leader, as child is
born of parents, but inversely; for it is as if these children create their father. The Self or psyche is a community or orchestra, poised under the baton of its
leader or conductor. The leader is part of the truth of
the community, in regard to which the visible and
conscious self is required to conform.

The composition to be played by each one of us is
our own Destiny: it is our own true tune in Time. The
orchestra, with its individual differences, represents
the many parts of self, the different instruments of
body and of mind. These create a whole, which is manifest in the conductor, as the unseen is shrouded by the
seen. Thus 'I AM' is played, for well or ill, through Me.

Is he then so free as he feels himself to be, to choose
his tune, or play his part according to his own choice
of time? Or is the power with which he feels himself
to be possessed a function of the community, a sum-
total derived from the members of his orchestra, not-
'withstanding' and 'in the circumstances'? If he plays
according to his taste another tune and time, while the
orchestra are bound to play their music according to
their truth, the end is discord. His power is his, only
if he represents the invisible conductor or unseen 'over-
soul' of his community, and if he plays the music as it
has been written, laid down in the laws of Time. Conductor is what he seems to be: but he must learn the
limits of that role, for he is conducted, too.

303

WISDOM

We are conductor and conducted, both: there is no escape from this duality of our dilemma. On both sides of the river, we must move and be moved: as flowers, growing and expanding that life may flow more freely through us: free and yet bound by unseen law: fertilizing, fertilized: male and female: past and future: seen and unseen: child and parent: one and many: there is no truth in life which is not born of this duality, NOW.

APPENDIX ON DREAMS
(*N.B. All remarks are only provocative.*)

I. '*The Learned Knife*'
Pear: fruit of the tree of knowledge.
Worm: seed of power.

II. '*Contrast*'
Earth/water is a well-known couple in dreams for male/female, or matter/spirit, or conscious/unconscious. We live upon the shore, between these two: unsure.

Heaven/Hell; why of course we should prefer Heaven! She does not seem very well. How odd that she should disagree with me.

III. '*The Time-Track*'
Paradise; where is Satan?

Black sheep; sheep and goats; black goats; black kids.

The railway line; movement; time; Satan. (This woman had vowed she would never grow up.) Alarm-clock; Time again; alarm! this time.

It is so much more convenient to fill time with work; 'Good gracious me, you're wasting time!'

APPENDIX ON DREAMS

IV. *'Snakes'*

Altogether too high; levels are important; obscenity is only a matter of wrong levels; the snake (power) belongs deep.

V. *'Privilege'*

The shore again; the measure of bombardment is the same measure as that of flight from the unseen. We make our enemies by running away from them. Reality is not 'it', but our attitude to 'it'. Flight requires privilege, and privilege, flight. A vicious circle.

VI. *'The Tempest'*

How clever that would be! And so reasonable too. Moral, once fixed, keep it fixed, or . . . be a millionaire.

VII. *'Garden of Eden'*

This tempting fruit.

Genesis, with unimportant changes.

Mackintosh; to keep the rain off, of course. The Handsome Policeman; is this Satan or God? Dancing; rhythm; time (this is the same dreamer as 'The Time-Track'). How could she be other than locked out of life?

VIII. *'Woolworths'*

'Consider the lilies'; they are synthetic!

If you knew her, you would know this was true; but only the dreamer would dare to tell her so.

IX. *'The Prize-Winner'*

This from a diehard intellectual, a schoolmaster by profession.

APPENDIX ON DREAMS

X. *'Black Magic'*
Too easy.
The fish should be enormous, as denizen of the deep.
(cf. ichthus).

XI. *'Up and Up'*
Fear of falling is the measure of unbalanced ambition.
The dreamer, like all true women, is both vulgar and matter of fact.

XII. *'Up and Down'*
(This series of five dreams all occurred within a week, but are the product of five different dreamers at different stages of treatment.)
(a) She is not yet ready for open water, and prefers the shelter of harbour and mother.
(b) Mental gymnastics up in the air; we must all be prepared to turn this somersault of paradox sometime; but alas for the abyss!
(c) Suspense; the bridge; only for one. The woman (female psyche) knows where she belongs. This is not suicide, but a truth realized. She is not to be joined, but the gulf is to be bridged.
(d) Going down slowly and more in detail; a sticky business. These girls seem to know everything.
Discussion is usually discouraging; flight from fact, it takes the place of spontaneous action.
(e) We are off, 'in spite of', rather than 'because'; with Father Time, or Charon to help us in between. Well, well!

INDEX

309

INDEX

310

INDEX

311

INDEX

INDEX

313

INDEX